THE SPACE EXPLORER'S GUIDE TO

Space Travel

BY **ANDREA GOLLIN**

WITH **RACHEL CONNOLLY**
SPACE EDUCATOR

RYAN WYATT
VISUAL ADVISOR

AND **JIM SWEITZER**, Ph.D.
NASA SCIENCE CENTER,
DePAUL UNIVERSITY

SCHOLASTIC INC.

NEW YORK   TORONTO   LONDON   AUCKLAND   SYDNEY
MEXICO CITY   NEW DELHI   HONG KONG   BUENOS AIRES

Who's Who at Space U

Andrea Gollin
Writer

Andrea is a writer who lives in Florida. She writes fiction and nonfiction for adults and children.

Rachel Connolly
Consultant

Rachel manages the astrophysics education program at the American Museum of Natural History's Rose Center for Earth and Space.

Ryan Wyatt
Visual Advisor

Ryan designs scientific visuals for the American Museum of Natural History's Rose Center for Earth and Space.

Jim Sweitzer
Advisor

Jim is an astrophysicist and the director of the NASA Space Science Center at DePaul University in Chicago.

With Special Thanks to:

Joy Barckholtz, Robert Curbeam, Paul Dye, Janet Kavandi, Kacy Kossum, Mike Gentry, Gloria Sanchez, and Tim Reynolds at NASA's Johnson Space Center. Also thanks to Marianne Dyson for all of her assistance.

ISBN: 0-439-55740-2

Copyright © 2003 by Scholastic Inc.

Editor: Andrea Menotti
Designers: Lee Kaplan, Peggy Gardner, Tanja Pohl, Robert Rath
Illustrators: Yancey C. Labat, Ed Shems, Paul Tutrone
Chinese calligraphy: Garrick Ho

Photos: All photos supplied by NASA unless otherwise noted.
Front cover: The space shuttle Discovery in orbit.
Back cover: An astronaut floats above Earth, wearing a SAFER (Simplified Aid for EVA Rescue)
pack that allows him to maneuver around by firing gas jets.
Page 5: Science Photo Library/Photo Researchers. Page 15: (Laika) AP Photo/NASA. Page 17: (Salyut) ITAR/TASS.
Page 46: (Orbital Space Plane) Orbital Sciences Corporation. Page 47: (Hyper-X) Media Fusion, Inc/NASA.
Page 48: (Mars) NASA/StScl/Colorado/Cornell/SSI, (Moon) NASA/JPL/USGS, (Shuttle) NASA photo by Carla Thomas.

12 11 10 9 8 7 6 5 4 3 2   3 4 5 6 7 8/0

Printed in the U.S.A.

First Scholastic printing, November 2003

The publisher has made every effort to ensure that the activities in this book are safe when done as instructed. Adults should provide guidance and supervision whenever the activity requires.

Table of Contents

3...2...1...

*C*adet, Mission Control.

Cadet, Mission Control, how do you copy?

Comm check...

Cadet, Mission Control, in the blind, you are go for space travel training...

Close and lock your visor and have a good flight!

Well, cadet, how do you copy? Are you go for space travel training? Is your visor closed and locked?

Not sure what all this means?

Not to worry! After this month's training, you'll know exactly how to respond to Mission Control, *and* you'll have the answers to questions like these:

How do rockets blast off into space?

What makes a spacecraft orbit around the Earth?

Why do astronauts float in space?

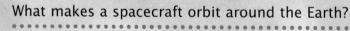

What's a vomit comet?

Do astronauts wear *diapers*?

Can you eat shrimp cocktail in orbit?
What about scrambled eggs? Chocolate pudding?

What might future spacecraft look like...
and where in the universe would *you* want to go?

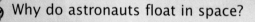
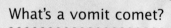

Liftoff!

This month's Space U training is all about how humans (as in Space U cadets, maybe someday!) can venture into space. But before you blast off, let's make sure you're clear on the mission objective.

WHAT'S THE POINT OF SPACE TRAVEL?

Here's a simple answer: We go to space to learn! We can bring equipment into space (like satellites and telescopes) to help us learn about our universe and our home planet. We can also conduct experiments up there to find out what it would be like for humans to live in space for long periods. Plus, technology developed in space has been used for all kinds of useful things on Earth—everything from life-saving medicines to lighter racing bikes!

Oh, and let's not forget the *other* big reason we travel to space: because it's *human nature*. That's right—it's part of human nature to want to explore a new frontier, to ask and answer big questions, and to keep learning and doing new things. As the Russian rocket scientist Konstantin Tsiolkovsky said, in 1911: "The Earth is the cradle of humanity, but one cannot live in the cradle forever."

Konstantin Tsiolkovsky (sy-ul-KOV-skee) (1857-1935), a Russian scientist and teacher, used math and physics to figure out how rockets could make it into space. Although he never built any rockets, he laid the groundwork for modern space travel. He believed strongly that people should not only travel to space, but live there.

WHERE DO WE USUALLY GO?

Astronauts on board NASA's space shuttle usually orbit about 200 miles (322 km) above the Earth. They also visit the International Space Station, which orbits about 240 miles up (386 km). To get a basic sense of this, grab a basketball, pretend it's the Earth, and measure a quarter of an inch (6 mm) from its surface with a ruler. That's how high astronauts usually go! Really! The Moon, on the other hand, would be about 23 feet (7 m) away from the basketball Earth. We went to the Moon many times in the 1960s and 1970s, but not since. The space shuttle doesn't even have enough power to make the trip!

Well, cadet, do you think we should plan another trip to the Moon? And where *else* do you think we should go? That's for you to think about as you start your training in space travel!

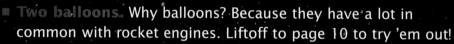

This month's Space Case is packed with stuff that'll make your space travel training a real blast! You've got:

- **A rocket launcher with two foam rockets.** The two rockets have an important difference, and it's not just color! Can you spot it? Fly to page 13 to get the answer—*and* to get your rockets airborne!

- **Two balloons.** Why balloons? Because they have a lot in common with rocket engines. Liftoff to page 10 to try 'em out!

- **A length of string and a plastic tube.** You'll use these handy tools to launch your balloon rockets and make a model of an orbit (see page 22).

- **A shuttle glider.** This paper spacecraft is a replica of NASA's space shuttle. Glide over to page 21 to start construction!

- **Freeze-dried astro-bananas.** What happens when bananas get prepped for space travel? Find out on page 38!

THE SPACE UNIVERSITY WEB SITE

There are lots of new games and space challenges on the Space U web site (www.scholastic.com/space) this month, so pay a visit...or two...or three! The secret password is right here on Planet Password.

PLANET PASSWORD

This month's web site password is:

LAUNCHTIME

Earn your personalized mission patch by completing the games and challenges on this month's Space U web site. Then print out the patch, cut it out, and paste it here!

If you want to make it into space, cadet, you're going to need something *very* powerful to get you and your Space Case above the Earth. That something is a rocket, the real *thrust* behind any space mission.

Rockets have been around for almost 800 years, but they didn't start cruising into space until the twentieth century. What were they up to before then? Well, let's just say it's not a very *peaceful* story, but here goes....

ROCKET BACK IN TIME!

The first rockets in recorded history were "fire arrows" used as weapons by the Chinese in the thirteenth century. Powered by burning "black powder" (gunpowder), these rockets rumbled like thunder as they streaked through the sky, and when they landed, they set the ground on fire! Not surprisingly, the idea spread like *wildfire*, and soon the Chinese invention started making its way around the world. In the centuries that followed, rockets got better and better (or worse, depending on which side of the rocket you were on!).

During the first half of the twentieth century, scientists in the United States, Germany, and the Soviet Union (a country that's now broken up into many smaller countries, including Russia) made big strides in rocketry. American rocket scientist Robert Goddard (whom you'll meet on page 8) launched the world's first *liquid-fueled* rocket in 1926. Liquid fuel produces more energy than solid fuel, and its flow can be controlled (turned off or slowed down)—so this was a very important advance.

Chinese rockets are just like modern-day fireworks.
Do you see the Chinese writing on this page?
It says "rocket"!

Then the Germans came up with their enormous V-2 rocket (or "missile"), also powered by liquid fuel, which they used to bomb targets during World War II (1939–1945).

After the war, German rocket scientists went to the United States and the Soviet Union to work on bigger, more long-range missiles. One Soviet rocket scientist named Sergei Korolëv had his mind set on putting a satellite on top of a big missile and launching it into space. When he succeeded, in 1957, in launching a tiny satellite called *Sputnik* into orbit, the world was completely shocked and amazed. Soon, the Americans and the Soviets were racing to see who could pull off the *next* most impressive feat in space. This race was called (guess what?) the Space Race, and you can read all about it on page 15.

Sputnik

wow!

Developed during the 1940s, the German V-2 was the largest and most advanced rocket in the world. It could fly 200 miles (322 km) in five minutes!

✳Astrotales

Robert Goddard, the Father of Modern Rocketry

Robert Goddard (1882–1945)

"The dream of yesterday is the hope of today and the reality of tomorrow."
—Robert Goddard

Robert Goddard was born in 1882, long before most people believed that space travel was possible. But from the time he was a boy growing up in Massachusetts, Goddard dreamed of exploring the solar system. He read science-fiction classics like H.G. Wells's *War of the Worlds* and Jules Verne's *From the Earth to the Moon*, and they filled his imagination with ideas. As he got older, he became a physics professor and started experimenting with rockets. Some of his ideas were considered a little crazy at the time, so people made fun of him. Because he talked about sending rockets to the Moon, he was called "the Moon man."

Then, on March 16, 1926, Goddard launched the first-ever liquid-fueled rocket, which he named Nell, from a field on his aunt's farm. During its 2.5-second flight, the rocket reached a height of 40 feet (12 m) and traveled a distance of 184 feet (56 m).

Despite this success, people still made fun of Goddard. A few years later, when he launched another rocket, the local newspaper's headline read, "Moon Rocket Misses Target by $238,799\frac{1}{2}$ Miles."

That didn't stop Goddard, who kept working... and working...and working. He made big advances in rocket science, developing many of the techniques that would later help take astronauts to the Moon.

Sadly, Goddard died in 1945, before rockets ever made it into space. Today, NASA's Goddard Space Flight Center in Maryland is named after him, and he's widely known as the father of modern rocketry.

Robert Goddard standing next to his first liquid-fueled rocket.

How Do Rockets Work?

Excellent question, cadet! Here's your answer: It's all about *forces*. Not police forces, not air forces, just plain old forces, or *pushes* and *pulls*.

THE GRAVITY OF THE SITUATION

When it comes to rockets, the most important force to consider is *gravity*. You've had plenty of experience with gravity—whenever you drop something, you're seeing Earth's gravity at work, pulling stuff down to the ground. Rockets have to be powerful enough to *overcome* the pull of Earth's gravity in order to make it into space.

ACTION...REACTION!

How do rockets get the force they need to battle against gravity? To find out the answer to this question, you'll need to meet Isaac Newton, a super-brainy English scientist from the seventeenth century. He came up with this big idea:

> For every action, there is always an equal and opposite reaction.

Isaac Newton (1642–1727)

This means that when something makes a force in *one* direction, there's an equal force made in the *opposite* direction. You can see these actions and reactions all around you. If you're wearing roller skates and you push someone forward, you'll roll backward. If you sit on a chair, you push down on it, and it pushes right back up on you (if it didn't, then you would keep going— straight to the floor)!

For rockets, there are burning gasses that rush out the bottom of the rocket, causing the rocket to move up. So the *action* is gas coming out of the engine. The *reaction* is...liftoff!

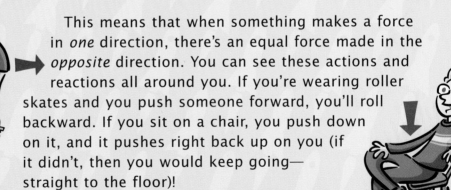

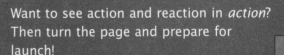

Want to see action and reaction in *action*? Then turn the page and prepare for launch!

IT IS ROCKET

So you've met Isaac Newton, and you've heard all about his law of action and reaction (turn back a page if you haven't!). Sounds like you're ready to launch your career in rocket science, cadet! Grab the balloons from your Space Case and let's...celebrate! No, seriously, let's launch some rockets!

Launch Objective

> Put Newton to the test by launching your own balloon rockets.

Your equipment

- Balloons
- Plastic tube
- String
- Tape
- Ruler or tape measure
- Launch Log or notebook
- Pencil

Personnel

- An Intergalactic Adult (IGA) to help with Part 3

Mission Procedure

Part 1: Ready, Action!

1 First of all, just blow up one of your balloons and let it go. WOOOSH!

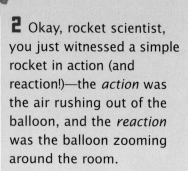

2 Okay, rocket scientist, you just witnessed a simple rocket in action (and reaction!)—the *action* was the air rushing out of the balloon, and the *reaction* was the balloon zooming around the room.

3 But if you were an astronaut, would you hitch a ride on a rocket like that? No way! That's why you're going to get some control over your rocket in the next part of this mission. To get ready for Part 2, rocket over to this month's Space University web site (www.scholastic.com/space) and print out your Launch Log pages. Or, if you prefer, you can use your own notebook instead.

Part 2: String Along

1 Grab two chairs and put them about 10 feet (3 m) apart.

2 Thread the string through the plastic tube.

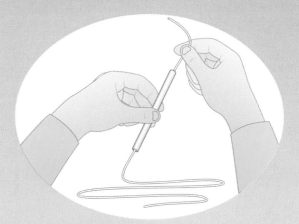

3 Tie or tape each end of the string securely to one of the chairs. Make sure the string is really tight.

4 Blow up one of the balloons and pinch it closed. Hold on tight (until step 7)!

SC1ENCE!

5 Tape the balloon onto the plastic tube with the open end facing away from the direction you want the rocket to travel.

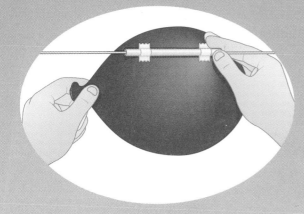

6 Slide the balloon to one end of the string and start the countdown. 3...2...1...

7 Liftoff! Let the balloon go!

8 How far did the rocket travel? Did it reach the other end of the string? Try launching your rocket again, but this time, put *less* air inside the balloon. What do you notice?

NOTE: Don't untape the balloon each time you blow it up, because you might make a hole in the balloon. Just blow up the balloon while it's taped to the tube.

9 Now get scientific! *Measure* how far your rocket travels when you fill it with just *one* puff (or breath) of air. Record the distance in your Launch Log or notebook. Try this a couple of times to see if you get the same distance (try to keep your puffs the same size each time!).

10 Try filling the balloon with *two* puffs of air, then *three*. Measure the distance the rocket travels each time. See how well you can control the action and reaction!

Part 3: Go Vertical!

1 With help from an IGA, tape one end of your rocket string to the ceiling. Tape the other end of the string to the floor. Just like before, make sure the string is really tight.

2 Blow up your balloon, pinch it closed, and tape it to the tube with the open end facing the floor. 3...2...1...

3 Liftoff!

4 How high did your rocket climb? Did it hit the ceiling? If not, try blowing up the balloon with *more* air than before, and see if you can make your rocket go all the way up to the top of the string.

5 Now compare! Can your rocket travel as far as it did in Part 2, when you use the same amount of air?

6 Measure the distance your rocket travels on *one* puff, *two* puffs, and *three* puffs of air power. To make your measurements, watch the launch, and put your finger on the highest point your rocket reaches before it falls back down. Have your IGA help you measure if the rocket gets too high for you to reach, and make sure to record your results in your Launch Log or notebook.

Science, Please!

So, cadet, did action and reaction work to your *satisfaction*? In Part 1, the rocket's flight was out of control because the open end of the balloon (where all the *action* is!) kept pointing in different directions. Remember what Newton said—the *reaction* will always be in the opposite direction from the *action*, so if you want to keep your rocket under control, you have to keep the *action* pointing in the right direction.

In Part 2, you should have found that the more you blew up the balloon, the farther it went. That's because you were giving your rocket more *thrust* (that's the rocket scientist word for the *action* power of the rocket). In Part 3, your rocket had to battle against the pull of gravity, so it shouldn't have traveled as far on the same amount of thrust as it did in Part 2.

Now imagine a huge, heavy rocket being launched straight up into the sky. Think of how much thrust *that* rocket needs to fight gravity's pull and still go so high!

More from Mission Control

Give your rocket a boost! Tape a *second* balloon to the other side of the tube (you'll need some help holding both balloons shut while you do this!). Can your rocket climb higher now?

PUMP IT UP!

Balloon rockets are great for testing out action and reaction, but you need a string to keep them controlled while they fly—and we all know *real* rockets don't fly into space on strings! If you want to see how rockets *really* fly, you have to let 'em soar, no strings attached! That's what your foam rockets are for. Try out this mission to see how you can *pump up* your rocket expertise!

Launch Objective

> Find out how different factors (like fin shape, launch angle, and weight) affect a rocket's flight.

Your equipment

- **Foam rockets and launcher** SPACE Case
- **An object to mark your launch pad**
- **Small pieces of paper or other small objects to mark where your rockets land**
- **Tape**
- **Penny**

Mission Procedure

Part 1: Fun with Fins

1 Go outside and find an open space that's fairly flat and *not* near a street.

2 Place one of the rockets (blue or yellow—your choice!) on the end of the launcher and pull the bottom tube out. Keep your other hand on the round bulging part of the launcher so you don't get your fingers caught when you push the tube back in.

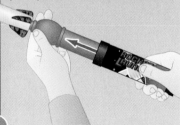

3 When the area's clear and you're ready for launch, push the tube back in, REALLY HARD! Liftoff!

4 Now try the other rocket. The blue rocket has *straight* fins and the yellow rocket has *angled* fins. Do you notice a difference in the way the two rockets fly? Try

launching both rockets a couple of times until you see the difference. You'll find the answer in "Science, Please!"

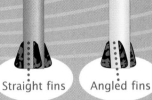

Straight fins   Angled fins

Part 2: Angle Action

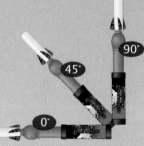

1 How should you angle your launch to make your rocket fly the farthest? Find out! Here are some angles for you to try. They're measured in *degrees* (0 degrees is flat; 90 degrees is straight up, and 45 degrees is exactly in between).

Which angle do you think will make your rocket fly the farthest?

2 Find a place that'll be your launch pad. Mark it with some object (like a book, a shoe, or a line of tape) so you remember where it is.

3 Choose *one* of the two rockets (the one you think flies the best) to use for all your launches.

4 Practice launching the rocket at a 0 degree angle a couple of times. Try to point the rocket in the exact same direction each time, and push in the bottom tube with the same amount of force. Keep trying until you get the rocket to land in pretty much the same place every time.

5 Place a marker (like a small piece of paper or tape) on the spot where the rocket lands.

6 Repeat steps 4 and 5 for the other two launch angles. Which angle gets you the most distance?

Part 3: A Penny For Your Payload

Now that you're an expert launcher, try attaching a *payload* to your rocket. A payload is the cargo a rocket carries into space (like a satellite or a space telescope). In your case, you'll take a penny for a rocket ride.

1 Tape a penny to the side of your rocket.

2 Launch the rocket at your favorite angle, and see how far it flies. Did it get as far as it did (at that launch angle) in Part 2?

3 Experiment with taping the penny in different places on the rocket. Try taping it on the bottom of the rocket, and then on the very top. Which placement gives you the best flight?

← **Most Distance!** **#1**

Nice Try!

In Part 1, did you notice that the yellow rocket's angled fins made it *spin* during flight? You probably noticed that the yellow rocket flew farther than the blue one, right? That's because the spinning motion helps stabilize the rocket during its flight, so it stays right on course.

As for launch angle, the 45 degree angle should have given you the most distance. Look at the rocket *trajectories* (or flight paths) below to see why. If you launch the rocket at 0 degrees, it'll hit the ground before it gets very far. With a 45 degree angle, the added height allows the rocket to travel farther before gravity pulls it down to Earth. If you want to launch your rocket for the most *height*, then straight up (90 degrees) is the launch angle for you. This is the launch angle that rockets use to get all the way up into space.

As for payload, can you see why rockets are designed to be as lightweight as possible? Putting the penny on the very *top* of the rocket should have resulted in the best flight.

#1 Most Height! →

90°

45°

0°

CONFESSIONS OF A FOAM ROCKET

Cadet, your foam rocket has a confession to make: It's not really a rocket. Did you notice? A *real* rocket is propelled by stuff firing out the back of it. You know, action and reaction, like your balloon rockets! The foam rocket flies through the air because it gets a big *push* of air from the rocket launcher, kind of like a cannonball blasting out of a cannon, or an arrow flying from a bow. But that's okay—your foam rocket still flies *like* a rocket, and you can still learn a lot about rocket flight from it!

During the 1950s and 1960s, the United States and the Soviet Union (which is now split up into a bunch of countries including Russia) raced against each other to see who could accomplish the most awe-inspiring feats in space. This very important time in space history was called (drum roll, please) the Space Race!

THE SPACE RACE ...AND BEYOND

Who won the Space Race, you ask? There's no simple answer to that question. Let's tune in to hear the highlights of the Space Race from our expert space commentators, **Ivana Flyarocket** and **Seymour Space**. Ivana is from the Soviet Union and Seymour is from the United States, and sometimes they get a little...well...caught up in the Space Race.

Ivana   Seymour

1957

Sputnik 1

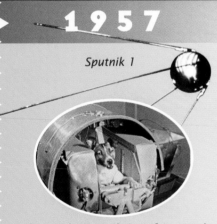

Laika inside *Sputnik 2*. Unfortunately, she did not survive her trip.

Ivana Flyarocket The Soviets lead the Space Race! They took the world by surprise when they launched *Sputnik 1*, the world's first satellite, on top of a giant rocket.

Seymour Space You call that a score?! That little metal ball isn't even two feet across! It's puny!

Ivana Now Seymour, don't be picky! *Sputnik 1* is a major achievement! It orbits Earth every 96 minutes, and its two radio transmitters send beeping signals back to us. Oh, this is just in... *Sputnik 2* launched, only a month after *Sputnik 1*. The dog Laika is onboard, which makes her the first live creature to travel into space.

1958

Explorer 1

Seymour *Now* we're talking! The U.S. just launched its first satellite, *Explorer 1*. It had scientific instruments aboard that discovered a radiation belt around the Earth!

1959

Luna 2

Ivana Listen to this! The Soviets have been launching a series of *Luna* spacecrafts. *Luna 2* landed on the surface of the Moon, and *Luna 3* orbited *around* the Moon and took photos of its far side. Wow!

Seymour Well, la-di-da. You neglected to mention that *Luna 2* *crash*-landed on the Moon. And besides, *I* won't be impressed until I see *people* in space...

1961

When Yuri Gagarin's rocket lifted off, he shouted "Payekhali!" ("Let's go!" in Russian). He was the first *cosmonaut* (that's the word for a Russian astronaut).

Ivana Spectacular spacedoodles! I don't believe it! I mean, I *do* believe it! The Soviet Union has just sent the first man into space! On April 12, Yuri Gagarin orbited Earth in one hour and forty-eight minutes.

Seymour And the United States matches that less than a month later, sending astronaut Alan Shepard into space.

Ivana Right, but his trip lasted for only fifteen measly minutes.

Seymour Well, we're getting there. In fact, President John F. Kennedy announced this year that the United States will put a man on the Moon by the end of the decade.

1962

John Glenn

Seymour In February, the United States sent the first American into orbit. The astronaut, John Glenn, spent about four and a half hours in space and orbited Earth three times. During his time in space, Glenn took photos through a tiny window and ate applesauce squeezed out of a tube! This was part of NASA's Mercury program that sent six astronauts into space.

Glenn's spacecraft, a capsule called *Friendship 7*, was launched atop this *Atlas* rocket.

1965

Ivana Have you heard? The Soviets just scored with the first space walk, made in March 1965 by Aleksei Leonov.

Seymour He sure looks funny in that space suit.

Ivana Oh, please! Think of how much guts it took to be the first person to venture out of a spacecraft, into empty space!

Aleksei Leonov was the world's first space-walker. "I felt absolutely free, soaring like a bird," Leonov said.

1969

Ivana The decade is almost over, and the Americans still haven't made it to the Moon. What's taking so long?

Seymour Ivana, are you crazy?! We've made great strides, and...and...Ivana, I don't believe it! We did it! On July 20, *Apollo 11* astronaut Neil Armstrong became the first human to set foot on the Moon!

Ivana Seymour, I have to admit it. I'm impressed.

Apollo 11 astronaut Buzz Aldrin on the surface of the Moon

1971

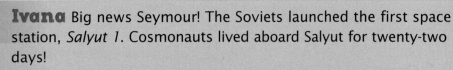

Salyut 1

Ivana Big news Seymour! The Soviets launched the first space station, *Salyut 1*. Cosmonauts lived aboard Salyut for twenty-two days!

Seymour But the craft didn't have much luck...it fell back down to Earth within the year.

Ivana But still, it was a first!

1973

Skylab

Seymour Now *this* is some promising news: The United States just launched *Skylab*, America's first space station. Astronauts can spend up to eighty-four days in orbit and do experiments.

1975

Ivana Look at this, Seymour. The Americans and the Soviets are cooperating! An American spacecraft and a Soviet spacecraft docked in space and the crews shook hands! Imagine that! I think the Space Race as we know it is over. Done! Kaput!

The American *Apollo* capsule (left) docks with the Soviet *Soyuz* spacecraft.

1981

Seymour Ivana, the Space Race may be old news, but we're still making great strides. This year, the United States launched the first space shuttle—a reusable launch system that can complete a hundred missions. It launches like a rocket, but when it comes back to Earth, it lands like an airplane!

The space shuttle *Atlantis*

1986

Ivana This just in: The Soviets have launched *Mir*, a new space station where cosmonauts will live and work for many months. The name "Mir" means "peace" and "community" in Russian.

Seymour Nice name! How do you say it? *Mur*?

Ivana Oh, Seymour. Learn some Russian! It's "*Meer*."

Mir remained in orbit for fifteen years. Some cosmonauts lived aboard for more than a year. American astronauts also visited for months at a time.

1998

The International Space Station

Seymour And here's more good news: the International Space Station (ISS) was launched this year. The United States, Russia, Japan, Canada, Italy, and several other countries are working together to build the ISS a little at a time.

Ivana Well, now that we're all working together, I predict that we'll accomplish even more great things!

Seymour Ivana, for once I have to agree with you! But it's just this once!

SHUTTLE Me UP!

Cadet, imagine getting a new car every time you went on a trip! That sounds crazy, right? But before NASA's space shuttle was invented, that's what we did for space travel—each spacecraft could be used once, and only once!

Space shuttles, on the other hand, were designed to make at least a hundred trips. A shuttle can carry tons of equipment and up to seven astronauts—it's like a space delivery truck and passenger bus in one! Check out the picture below to take a quick tour of the shuttle's main features.

Main Engines

These provide some of the thrust the shuttle needs during launch (the solid rocket boosters provide the rest).

Multi-Purpose Logistics Module

This module is a frequent flier on the shuttle because it holds racks of experiments and supplies for the International Space Station. The shuttle's robotic arm lifts the module out of the cargo bay and attaches it to the space station so it can be unloaded (and then reloaded with equipment no longer needed on board the station).

Orbital Maneuvering System

These engines are used to get the shuttle into its final orbit. They're also used to slow the shuttle down for reentry into Earth's atmosphere.

Wings

The shuttle has wings so it can land like an airplane.

Cargo Bay Doors

These are kept open while the shuttle is in space. That's because the inside surfaces of the doors have radiators that help keep the shuttle cool by letting heat escape into space.

The Shuttle Stack

The Space Transportation System (STS) has three main parts: the orbiter (often called the "shuttle"), the external fuel tank, and the solid rocket boosters.

Orbiter

The orbiter holds all of the astronauts and cargo. As you can tell from its name, it's the part that goes into orbit.

External Fuel Tank

The orbiter sits on top of a large, orange fuel tank that's filled with liquid hydrogen and oxygen.

Solid Rocket Boosters

On either side of the big orange tank there are solid rocket boosters. They're filled with solid rocket fuel that provides most of the thrust the shuttle needs during launch.

Flight Deck

The astronauts control the shuttle and operate the robotic arm from this part of the cabin, the front of which is called the "cockpit."

Robotic Arm

This robotic arm, designed by the Canadian Space Agency, can move equipment from the cargo bay, and it can serve as a moving work platform for astronauts on EVAs (extravehicular activities, or space walks).

Cargo Bay

This holds instruments and cargo like satellites and telescopes. The equipment that the shuttle carries into space is known as the "payload."

Middeck

This part of the cabin is the crew's living space. Astronauts work, eat, exercise, do their grooming, go to the bathroom, and sleep here.

Orbiter Docking System

This part is used to dock the shuttle to the International Space Station.

Fuel Cells

The shuttle's fuel cells create electricity to run the shuttle by converting liquid oxygen and hydrogen into water (which the astronauts drink) and energy. The shuttle will run out of this fuel in about two weeks, so it can't support long-term living in space!

LAUNCH TIME!

⑤ HIGHER ORBIT

About 45 minutes after launch, the shuttle's Orbital Maneuvering System (OMS) fires to raise the shuttle into a higher orbit. How high? It depends on the mission. The shuttle has gone as high as 385 miles (620 km) above Earth, but usually it goes to a height of 200 miles (322 km), where it whizzes around Earth about once every 90 minutes!

④ BYE-BYE, EXTERNAL FUEL TANK

After nine minutes, the empty external fuel tank separates from the orbiter. The external tank will not be reused; it burns up in the atmosphere as it plummets back to Earth.

③ MAIN ENGINE CUT-OFF

After about eight and a half minutes, the main orbiter engines stop burning—astronauts call it MECO, for Main Engine Cut-off. The shuttle is now 70 miles (113 km) above Earth's atmosphere.

② SEE YA LATER, SOLID ROCKET BOOSTERS

After about two minutes, the solid rocket boosters fall away and parachute down to the ocean where they are picked up to be reused for another launch.

① LIFTOFF!

At launch, the shuttle's main engines and solid rocket boosters ignite, lifting the shuttle off the launch pad.

The Risks of Space Travel

Although the space shuttle has been one of the most reliable space ships in history, space travel always has risks. Shuttles have completed more than a hundred successful missions, but on two occasions, shuttle missions ended in tragedy.

The space shuttle Challenger exploded during launch in January 1986 due to a leak in its external fuel tank. In February 2003, the space shuttle Columbia burned up during reentry into Earth's atmosphere. These tragedies revealed problems in the shuttle's design, which NASA then worked to repair. The loss of the crew members is not something that NASA or anyone can repair, but we *can* continue to press forward in our space explorations, which is what the crew members would have wanted.

BUILD YOUR OWN SHUTTLE GLIDER

So, you've seen what happens when a space shuttle launches... how does the shuttle *land*, you ask? It glides! Really! The shuttle glides halfway around the world on its way to landing—no engines involved. Try this mission to see a gliding shuttle (your own paper version, that is!) in action!

Launch Objective

Assemble and fly a space shuttle glider.

Your equipment

▶ Space shuttle glider
▶ Scissors
▶ Tape
▶ Glue (optional)

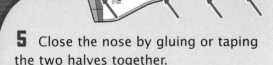

Mission Procedure

1 Cut out all the parts of the glider.

2 Cut the notches on the Fuselage and fold the tabs out.

3 Fold the Fuselage in half along the line running down its middle.

4 Place the Fuselage on top of the Deck and Wing Assembly and glue or tape down the tabs.

5 Close the nose by gluing or taping the two halves together.

6 Send the glider for a test flight. Hold it back near the wings and use a gentle, level toss to launch it. How does it fly?

7 Now fold the Vertical Stabilizer and attach it to the Fuselage. Match tab A with point A and tab B with point B. Tape the sides of the Vertical Stabilizer together so there's no gap between them.

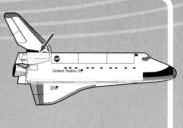

8 Fly the glider again. What do you notice this time?

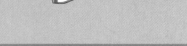

Science, Please!

Did you notice how much better the glider flies with the Vertical Stabilizer in place? Bet you didn't think a little piece of paper would make such a difference! But this vertical piece really *does* help stabilize the glider during flight.

How far did your shuttle glide? No matter what, it's not going to match up to the real thing—since the real shuttle glides for about 12,000 miles (19,300 km) before it touches down! That's right—at the end of the every mission, the shuttle enters Earth's atmosphere almost exactly on the opposite side of Earth from its landing site. It glides the whole way home, turning and tilting its wings to stay on course, before it touches down like an airplane on a runway.

More from Mission Control

Try taping a small paper clip to the nose of your glider. This weight should help balance the glider and allow it to fly even farther!

Mission

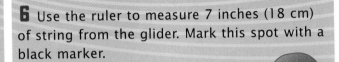

> Have you ever wondered how the space shuttle can orbit Earth and just keep on going around and around and around? Why doesn't the shuttle zoom off into space or fall back to Earth? And does the shuttle have to be steered in circles around the Earth, or are other forces at work that keep the shuttle on its path? Try this mission and find out!

Launch Objective

> Create a model of an orbit.

Your equipment

▶ Empty plastic water or soda bottle
▶ $\frac{3}{4}$ cup (18 cl) of water
▶ A small roll of clear tape
▶ 3 feet (1 m) of string
▶ Shuttle glider
▶ Plastic tube
▶ Ruler
▶ Black marker

Space Case

Mission Procedure

1 Fill the bottle with a small amount of water—about $\frac{3}{4}$ cup (18 cl). Screw the cap back on.

2 Tie one end of the string to the roll of tape.

3 Tape the shuttle glider onto the roll of tape.

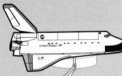

4 Slide the free end of the string through the plastic tube.

5 Tie the string around the neck of the bottle so there's about 30 inches (76 cm) of string between the shuttle and the top of the bottle.

6 Use the ruler to measure 7 inches (18 cm) of string from the glider. Mark this spot with a black marker.

7 Okay, you're ready to go into orbit! Stand up, and hold the plastic tube in one hand and the shuttle in the other. Keep the shuttle 7 inches (18 cm) away from the plastic tube, and let the bottle rest on the ground.

8 Slowly start moving the tube in small circles to get your shuttle moving around in an orbit. Try to keep the shuttle the same distance from the tube, using the black mark as a guide.

9 Once you have your shuttle spinning, you'll be able to lift the bottle off the ground. Try it! Just don't let your shuttle get pulled in toward the tube! Oh, and make sure to keep the spinning shuttle *away* from your face!

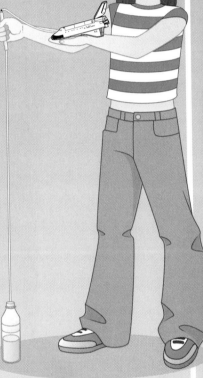

OR ELSE!

10 Keep spinning the shuttle at just the right speed to keep your orbit at the distance you marked with the black dot. Congratulations! You've achieved orbit!

More from Mission Control

Here's an extra challenge for you: Try adding more water to the bottle. What do you have to do to keep your shuttle orbiting at the right distance now?

Science, Please!

Your shuttle travels in an orbit because the weight of the bottle creates a force that pulls on the string. That pulling force keeps the shuttle going around and around your hand instead of flying off across the room.

The same thing is true for the *real* shuttle. When the real shuttle orbits around the Earth, Earth is like the bottle, and Earth's gravity acts like the string, pulling the shuttle toward Earth.

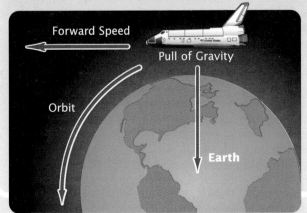

Forward Speed

Pull of Gravity

Orbit

Earth

No one has to steer the shuttle to keep it going in laps around the Earth. The shuttle just has to move forward *really* fast, and Earth's gravity will bend its path into a curved orbit.

Remember how you had to find just the *right* speed to keep your shuttle's orbit exactly at the distance you marked? If you went too slow, the shuttle started to get sucked in toward the tube.

This is true for the shuttle, too. The shuttle has to go forward at just the right speed—about 17,300 miles per hour (28,000 km/h)—in order to stay in its orbit.

But what keeps the shuttle going forward? You had to provide the spinning motion in your model, but the shuttle doesn't have to keep blasting its engines to stay up to speed. The shuttle got its speed from its rockets during launch, and since there's not much in space to slow it down, it just keeps going at that speed for the whole mission. When it's time to go home, the shuttle's commander slows the shuttle down and lets it fall back to Earth.

Did you try the More from Mission Control challenge? If you did, you should have found that, with more water in the bottle, you had to spin the shuttle faster to keep it orbiting at the right distance. That's because the heavier bottle is pulling down harder, so you have to make the shuttle move faster to balance this force. The same thing would happen if the shuttle were in orbit around a big planet like Jupiter—it would have to travel faster than it would at the same distance above Earth.

Part 2:
What's It Like Up There?

So, your rocket has carried you up into space, and now you're in orbit around Earth. What's it like? Well, first things first: You float! You can glide around your spacecraft just by pushing off a wall with a single finger. Is that because there's no gravity up there? A lot of people will answer "yes" to that question, but...

They're wrong!

And *you* can tell them why! Spread the word:

THERE *IS* GRAVITY UP THERE!

Remember the orbit model on pages 22–23? (Back up two pages if you haven't tried it!) What kept the spacecraft orbiting around Earth? That's right: GRAVITY! Without gravity, there would be no orbit. The spacecraft would just zoom off into space.

So why do astronauts float around in space? Because they're *falling*! That's right—everything in orbit is actually falling toward the Earth, thanks to the pull of gravity. And when you fall, you feel *weightless*.

What's that like? Well, if you've ever been on a roller coaster that dropped downhill really quickly, you probably felt yourself lift off your seat for a moment as you and the roller coaster car *fell* down the hill. That was a little taste of weightlessness! When you landed back on the seat, you felt your weight again.

The same thing happens to astronauts inside their spacecraft, except they just keep falling, and falling, and falling...the whole time they're in orbit! We call this *free fall*, since the astronauts (and their spacecraft) are falling with nothing to stop them.

What's *that* like? Well, imagine getting into a special space elevator. Suddenly, the floor drops from below you and you're falling...falling...falling...

But wait! You're not hitting the floor; you're not even getting any closer to the floor! That's a cool trick, cadet—how'd you do it? The secret is that the elevator is falling, too, just like you are. As long as it never stops, you'll never catch up to the floor. You'll float around the elevator, and you'll feel weightless because there's nothing below you holding you up. But is there still gravity? You bet, cadet! *That's* what's pulling you and the elevator down!

BUT IF SPACE SHIPS ARE FALLING, HOW COME THEY DON'T JUST FALL BACK TO EARTH?

Spacecraft don't fall back down to Earth because they're also moving *forward* so fast (about 17,000 miles, or 27,400 km, per hour!) that the Earth's surface curves away before the spacecraft can get any closer. It's a perfect balance between falling and moving forward!

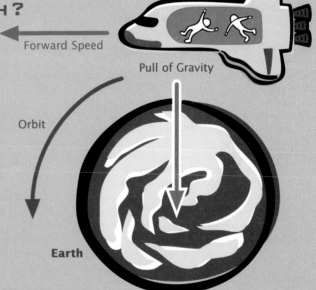

Forward Speed

Pull of Gravity

Orbit

Earth

Spacecraft have to go *really* fast to make it into orbit. Here's one way to think about that. What happens when you throw something as hard as you can? It flies away in a big curving path, but eventually gravity pulls it to the ground, *thud*. If you throw the ball even faster, it'll go even farther before it lands. Now imagine you have an amazing rocket arm, and you can throw a ball 17,000 miles an hour (27,400 km/h)! Then your ball will be able to go so far that the curve of the Earth will match the curved path of the ball, and it'll just keep going around and around, always falling, but never getting any closer to Earth!

WEIGHTLESS WONDERS

So, you've heard that astronauts are in free fall when they're in orbit, and that's what makes them float around. Want to see the effects of free fall for yourself? Then try this!

Launch Objective

▶ **Watch two astronauts become weightless in free fall!**

Your equipment

▶ **Half a letter-sized sheet of paper**
▶ **Tape or stapler**
▶ **15-inch piece of string** SPACE Case
▶ **Markers or colored pencils**
▶ **Empty 2-liter clear plastic soda bottle**

Mission Procedure

1 Fold the paper in half, and then in half again, and (one more time!) in half again. You should end up with a strip of paper about 1½ inches (4 cm) wide.

2 Tape or staple the edges of your paper strip so it stays together.

3 Draw two little astronauts on the strip using markers or colored pencils.

4 Tape or staple one end of the string to the top of the strip.

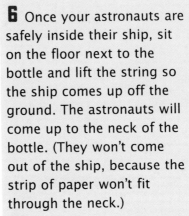

5 Carefully roll the strip and insert it into the soda bottle, making sure to keep the other end of the string from going into the bottle.

6 Once your astronauts are safely inside their ship, sit on the floor next to the bottle and lift the string so the ship comes up off the ground. The astronauts will come up to the neck of the bottle. (They won't come out of the ship, because the strip of paper won't fit through the neck.)

7 Let go of the string and watch what your astronauts experience on the way down!

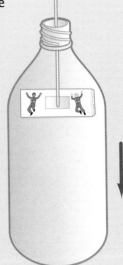

Science, Please!

When you dropped your soda bottle ship, your astronauts stayed at the top of the bottle while they were falling to the floor. That's because they were experiencing weightlessness! As they fell, the bottle was falling, too, so they could float freely...until the bottle hit the floor. Then the little astronauts quickly plummeted to the bottom of the ship (ouch!).

DRESS FOR SPACE SUCCESS

What kinds of clothes do you pack for space travel? Lots of different kinds! Each part of the mission has its own dress code. You wouldn't want to get dressed up in your space suit for a day of floating around the shuttle cabin, and you sure wouldn't want to step out for a space walk in your T-shirt and shorts. And for launch and landing? Better get decked out in your finest orange pressure suit!

Sound complicated? Never fear. The Department of Cosmic Fashion here at Space U will help make sure you're dressed for space success!

LAUNCH AND LANDING: PRESSURE SUITS

Astronauts wear orange pressure suits for space shuttle launches and landings. As you know, in space, there's no air—and as you get higher up into Earth's atmosphere, the air gets thinner and the air pressure gets weaker. Normally the shuttle cabin is *pressurized*, or pumped full of air at just the right pressure, but if there were ever a leak or a problem (which could happen if there were a mishap during launch or landing), the astronauts would be in trouble. Remember your Space Simulator from your first month at Space U? When you pumped the air out of the container, the stuff inside started to expand, right? Well, we wouldn't want an astronaut to experience anything like that! So, if there were ever a loss of air pressure inside the cabin, the suits would inflate and provide enough pressure for the astronauts to survive.

Helmet

The pressure suit's life raft.

The pressure suit also includes a parachute, a survival kit, and an inflatable life raft! Oh, and in case the astronauts have to go to the bathroom while they're waiting for launch or landing, they wear a diaper (or some other kind of "urine collection device") under the pressure suit so they can relieve themselves right away.

ON BOARD THE SHUTTLE

S ince the shuttle's cabin is pumped full of air and kept at just the right pressure, astronauts in orbit can wear clothes pretty much like the kind they'd wear on Earth—with a few important differences.

No shoes necessary! Astronauts just wear socks around the cabin.

Some astronauts wear more than one watch so they can keep track of "Mission Elapsed Time" (the time since launch) as well as the time at home, where their families are.

Astronauts can wear either shorts or pants, whichever they prefer. Some find it too cold on the shuttle for shorts.

Strips of Velcro on astronauts' pants keep tools and supplies close at hand (because you can't set something down and expect it to stay there!). Objects like clipboards, meal trays, tools, and books have Velcro strips on them so they can be attached to the pants.

Shirts often have the shuttle name or mission number on them.

Foot restraints hold astronauts in place while they're working.

Pants have deep pockets with flaps to keep things inside.

Suit Up
for a SPACEWALK!

In case the astronaut gets hungry or thirsty, the suit is stocked with a **chewy energy bar and a pouch of water** (to be sipped through a straw in the helmet).

The Primary Life-Support System provides air to breathe, water to cool the suit, electrical power, a fan for ventilation, and radio equipment. It can last for up to seven hours before it needs to be refilled and recharged.

Head lamps

The visor protects the astronaut's eyes from the Sun's glare. Inside the helmet, the astronaut wears a headset to communicate with the shuttle.

When it's time to venture *outside* of the spacecraft for an EVA (extravehicular activity), astronauts put on the ultimate space outfit: the Extravehicular Mobility Unit (EMU), otherwise known as the space suit. With fourteen layers of material, the space suit protects the astronaut from bits of flying space junk, and it keeps the temperature and air pressure inside just right. It's like a temporary, one-person, form-fitting spacecraft!

The SAFER (Simplified Aid for Extravehicular Rescue) allows the astronaut to return to the spacecraft (if a tether breaks) by blasting gas jets like a rocket.

Checklists are attached to the sleeve to help the astronaut remember procedures.

Displays and controls for the suit are on the astronaut's chest.

The astronaut's tools (used for building and repairing space equipment) are attached to the suit with cables.

The astronaut wears a diaper or another kind of "urine collection device" in case nature calls in the middle of a space walk.

The astronaut's feet are secured on the end of the shuttle's robotic arm.

Space Suit Underwear

Under the suit, the astronaut wears a garment that's like long underwear except it's lined with tubes. The space suit pumps cool water through these tubes, keeping the astronaut from getting too hot and sweaty.

Ready for More?

Now that you know how to get up there and what kinds of clothes to pack, it's time to begin your astronaut training!

Part 3:
Astronaut Training

Being an astronaut seems like a stellar job, right? You catch a ride on a rocket, float in space, build space stations, repair satellites, and conduct scientific experiments that help us learn more about the universe, biology, our planet—you know, little details like that!

But before all this comes training...*lots* of training!

HOW DO ASTRONAUTS TRAIN?

At NASA's Johnson Space Center in Houston, Texas, astronauts-in-training take classes and study textbooks to learn how the space shuttle's systems work. Then they get hands-on experience in a simulator—a model of the shuttle's cockpit that astronauts can use to practice their entire mission.

Astronauts also learn how to fly jets, and they're taught how to survive in the wilderness and in water (in case they have to eject out of an aircraft in trouble).

DIVE IN!

To practice their space walks or EVAs (extravehicular activities), astronauts head for the pool! Wearing special underwater space suits, they're lowered into a huge swimming pool with a life-sized model of the shuttle's cargo bay at the bottom. In order to make the water environment feel more like space, astronauts wear weights so they'll stay submerged instead of floating up to the surface. The astronauts are not actually weightless like they are in space, but the feeling is close enough to make it useful for practice.

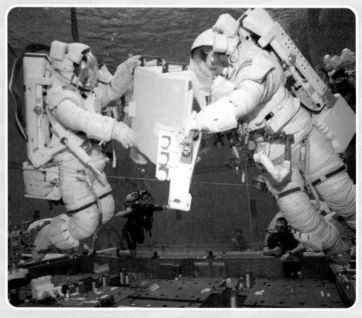

Underwater, astronauts can practice the repairs and installations they'll be performing in space.

VOMIT COMET!

Another way astronauts practice weightlessness is by flying aboard the "vomit comet." The vomit comet is an airplane that dives through the air, making the astronauts feel weightless for about twenty seconds on the way down. Unfortunately, it can also make them feel like losing their lunch! In fact, astronauts say that flying into space is *easier* on the stomach than a ride on the vomit comet!

Astronaut Mary Ellen Weber onboard the vomit comet, testing a device she'll use to stabilize herself while operating the shuttle's robotic arm.

QuickBlast

All Shook Up!

Most astronauts feel a little "space sick" when they first arrive in space. Want to know what space sickness feels like? There's an easy way to find out!

1 Close your eyes and spin in a circle about seven times.

2 Stop, and *don't* open your eyes.

3 Do you still feel like you're spinning? That's because you've confused your *vestibular system*—a network of fluid-filled canals inside your ears that maintain your sense of balance and help control your movements.

When you spin, the fluid in your vestibular system starts swirling, and it keeps on swirling for a while after you stop (like when you swirl a glass of water, and the water keeps sloshing around after you stop moving the glass). This means that your vestibular system tells your brain that you're still turning, even when you *know* that you aren't. The result? Barf bag city!

A similar thing happens in space—the vestibular system gets confused because it can no longer tell which way is up. This means that some astronauts feel dizzy and nauseous for their first few days in space. As they get used to the experience of weightlessness, the astronauts usually feel better.

ASTRONAUT TRAINER
Joy Barckholtz

Astronauts train in simulators—machines that look and act like the space shuttle. Space U talked to astronaut trainer Joy Barckholtz about the simulators. Joy has been working for NASA at the Johnson Space Center in Houston, Texas as an astronaut trainer for eighteen years.

Joy Barckholtz sits in the commander's seat on the space shuttle simulator.

Question: Can you describe the space shuttle simulator?

Answer: It's a life-sized version of the front portion of the space shuttle. The inside is the flight deck of the space shuttle, and everything is located just like on the shuttle. The computers are programmed to make the simulator act and move like the real shuttle. It can move in six different directions. The windows even show scenes of what you would see out the windows of the real shuttle, like the clouds going by and then the constellations!

Q: What does the simulator feel like?

A: We strap the astronauts in their seats. Then we rotate the simulator backwards so that they're lying with their legs above them, just like on the launch pad. At liftoff, the simulator shoots up into the air. It doesn't leave the ground, but it lifts up quickly. It feels like being on a gentle amusement park ride. When it comes in for landing, it tilts forward.

Q: How do you "break" the simulator?

A: We don't actually break pieces of equipment—we program the computers for malfunctions. For example, we can set up the computer so that a fuel line might leak or a piece of equipment stops working. We can even break the toilet! The crew has books of procedures that tell them step-by-step how to fix the problems.

Q: What are some of the most important rules you teach astronauts?

A: We encourage them to study hard and learn all they can. We also tell them that if they don't know the answer, don't make it up! Someone's life or safety may depend on having the right answer. And we tell them to make sure that they do great things and then come back and share their new knowledge with the world!

YOU TAKE THE CONTROLS!

The shuttle's flight deck has more than 2,000 displays and controls. Do you think you can make sense of all those buttons, switches, dials, knobs, gauges, and screens? Step into the simulator and find out!

Launch Objective

Take the controls of the space shuttle!

Your equipment

▶ Pencil
▶ Paper

Mission Procedure

1 Study the picture below, and see if you can figure out which control, gauge, display, or fixture you'd use for each of these tasks. Write the appropriate number next to each letter.

2 Check your answers on page 48!

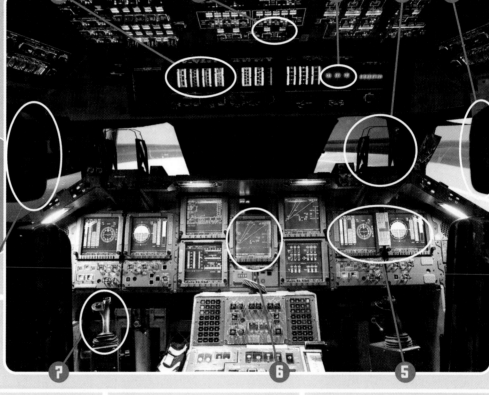

A Sit in the commander's seat. Which of the two seats will you take? (Hint: Look at the picture on page 32!)

B Check the "mission elapsed time" (the time since launch). The time is shown in hours, minutes, and seconds.

C Check the shuttle's fuel levels. (Hint: The shuttle has four different fuels.)

D Tilt the orbiter forward. To do this, find the "stick" that tilts the orbiter forward and back and rotates it side to side.

E The shuttle did not respond the way you expected when you moved the stick. Check that the RCS (Reaction Control System) jet switches are in the correct positions.

F Check to see if you're on your orbit path or not. Use this screen to see your *trajectory* (your path).

G It's time to land the shuttle. Look at these screens to see your compass direction, airspeed, and altitude as you glide through the air.

H You're about to touchdown on the runway! Check this "heads-up display" to get a 3-D view of the runway. The display is made of two glass screens held up by a metal support. It's useful because you can look at it and still see out the window.

ASTRONAUT Janet Kavandi

What makes people decide to be astronauts? And once they decide, how do they *launch* their careers? Space U talked with NASA astronaut Dr. Janet Kavandi about these and other questions.

On her three space shuttle missions, Dr. Kavandi orbited Earth 535 times and traveled more than 13 million miles. Like many astronauts, Dr. Kavandi has an advanced degree in science (which is why she has the title "Dr.").

During a mission in July 2001, Dr. Kavandi served as the robotic arm operator, carrying astronauts on the robotic arm from the shuttle to the space station. Here she is at the arm's control station.

Question: What made you decide to become an astronaut?

Answer: I have loved space since I was a kid. My dad and I liked to sit outside and look at all the stars and wonder what it would be like to see the Earth from space. When I got older, I decided that being an astronaut was what I wanted to do.

Q: What did you study in school?

A: I have a college degree in chemistry, and a Ph.D. in analytical chemistry. I also studied a lot of math in school.

Q: What kinds of things did you learn in astronaut training, and how long did it take?

A: We learned how to fly jets, use robotics, work in cumbersome spacesuits, and train in simulators. Basic training took about eighteen months. Once you're assigned to a mission, it takes about another year to train for the specifics of that mission.

Q: What was the hardest part of training?

A: I think that the most physically difficult part is training underwater for space walking. You wear a large white space suit that is pressurized to counteract the water pressure, so that makes the suit very stiff and difficult to maneuver. You learn how to operate heavy tools in the water, and you can be in the suit for six to eight hours at a time. When you get out, you're usually tired and hungry.

Q: What was the most important thing you learned in astronaut training?

A: There's nothing that's not important. There are many systems and emergencies that we train for that are critical to surviving in space, so a lot of time is spent on that type of training. However, the whole reason we go to space is for scientific gain, so science training is also very important.

Q: What advice do you have for a Space U cadet who wants to be an astronaut?

A: The important things are to do well on schoolwork and to set goals. Math and science are important for this job as well as medicine, engineering, and piloting. Other things that are important are learning to accept responsibilities and being a good team member, because on a space mission your actions affect the well-being and possibly the lives of the other people.

Q: How do you feel about the risks of space travel?

A: I feel honored to do what I have done and to have seen what I've seen, and I'm willing to accept the risks because I believe the benefits are worthwhile.

Part 4:
Life in Orbit!

No doubt, cadet, space travel is loads of fun—but it's hard work, too. Astronauts start working almost as soon as they float out of their sleeping bags in the morning, and they don't get much rest until they float back in at night.

SPACE WALK TO WORK

Astronauts who go on space walks—extravehicular activities (EVAs)—aren't out there to check out the view. They're out there because there are important jobs to do, like repairing satellites and space telescopes, testing space equipment, and attaching new parts to the International Space Station (ISS).

SCIENCE IN FREE FALL

Inside the shuttle, astronauts perform and monitor science experiments. They grow things like plants, crystals, and cancer cells to find out how

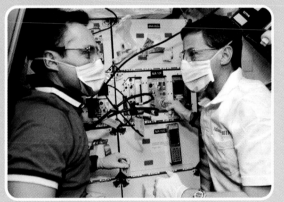

they respond to weightlessness. These experiments help us develop better medicines and technology for people on Earth, and they help us prepare to send people into space for long-term stays.

FLASH FACT

Space science also involves animals. Rats, monkeys, frogs, fish, jellyfish, crickets, and snails (among others!) have all flown into orbit as part of space research projects.

Who's Who on the Space Shuttle Crew?

Commander: The commander is responsible for the shuttle, the crew, and the mission's success.

Pilot: The pilot helps the commander operate the shuttle.

Mission Specialists: These astronauts perform space walks and have many responsibilities on the shuttle, including overseeing the experiments.

Payload Commander: This crew member is in charge of all the experiments and cargo for the mission.

Educator Astronauts: These are teachers who are trained to be mission specialists. They share their experiences with students and teachers across the country.

A DAY in the Life of an Astronat

Ask an astronaut what a typical day in space is like, and they'll tell you that there *is* no typical day. There are different tasks for each day of the mission. Here's an example of some of the tasks for shuttle commander Kent Rominger on April 29, 2001, when the space shuttle Endeavor undocked from the International Space Station (ISS).

Endeavor Schedule 04.29.2001

Commander: Kent Rominger

4:10–7:10 a.m. (Central Time)	After the astronauts wake up, they get ready for the day, eat breakfast, do some cleaning on the shuttle, and start work.
7:10–8:10 a.m.	The shuttle transfers oxygen to the ISS.
8:40–9:40 a.m.	The shuttle astronauts and the ISS crew share a last meal together before undocking.
9:40–10:10 a.m.	Official farewell ceremony between the shuttle crew and the ISS astronauts.
10:10–10:35 a.m.	The hatches between the space shuttle and the ISS are closed.
11:50 a.m.–1:40 p.m.	The shuttle undocks from the ISS. The undocking operations involve the whole shuttle crew. Some of the jobs they do include taking pictures of the ISS and measuring the distance between the shuttle and the ISS.
2:15–2:30 p.m.	The astronauts pack their equipment and put it in the crew cabin.
2:30–2:40 p.m.	Since this is the day before landing, the crew does a voice check with Mission Control to make sure communications are working properly.
2:40–2:55 p.m.	The shuttle's computer is programmed to complete a maneuver in the future (while the astronauts are asleep) that will turn the shuttle so its payload bay faces the Earth.
2:55–5:40 p.m.	The astronauts eat dinner and get ready for bed.
3:55–4:10 p.m.	Rominger has a private medical conference with the flight surgeons (doctors) in Mission Control.
5:40 p.m.–1:40 a.m. (the next day)	The astronauts are scheduled for eight hours of sleep each night.
1:10–1:25 a.m.	The shuttle maneuvers into position with the payload bay facing Earth while the astronauts are asleep.

So, you've reviewed the schedule for astronaut's day in space. Are you reato spend a day in orbit?

WAKE UP!

You'll start your day with wake-up music from Mission Control. Each morning, the song is dedicated to one of the astronauts. It could be anything from a Russian folk song to an Italian opera to a recent pop hit. What song would *you* want to wake *you* up in space?

OUT-OF-THIS-WORLD GROOMING TIPS

Grooming in space is just a *little* different from what you're used to on Earth.

Want to take a shower? Sorry, there is no shower! It would take up too much space. Instead, you'll have to clean yourself with a wet towel or sponge.

You can brush your teeth, no problem— but when it comes time to spit, you'll have to spit into a tissue (otherwise there'd be a gob of toothpastey spit floating around the cabin—yuck!).

Oh, and when it comes to hairstyling—*that* can get pretty wild. If you have long hair, better keep it tied back!

Talk about a bad hair day!

THE SPACED-OUT LOOK

Space makes you look different—your face gets puffy. That's because there's no up or down in space, so your body fluids don't get pulled down to the lower parts of your body (which is what happens on Earth). Instead, your body fluids spread *throughout* your body, making your face, chest, and arms bigger, and your legs skinnier. This is called *fluid shift*.

QuickBlast

Space Face

Want to find out what you'd look like in space? It's easy. Just grab a handheld mirror and lie down on your back on a bed or couch. Let your head hang upside down over the edge. Count to 60 and then hold the mirror in front of your face. Congratulations—you now have a puffy space face, thanks to the extra fluids that have rushed to your upside-down head!

LUNCH in Free Fall

Astronaut Loren Shriver snacks on floating peanut M & M's.

What's for lunch? Well, your food can't be crumbly (floating crumbs = big mess!), and it can't spoil, because there are no refrigerators or freezers. Some foods are space-worthy just as they are—like nuts and candy. But most foods have to be specially prepared for easy storage during space flight.

A lot of space food is dehydrated or *freeze-dried*, which means the water has been removed from it, like your astro-bananas. Without water, the food won't spoil, and it's lighter and easier to store. Foods like oatmeal, scrambled eggs, and even shrimp cocktail are dehydrated. Astronauts *rehydrate* the food by squirting water into the packages.

Freeze-dried shrimp cocktail is a favorite among astronauts for its spicy flavor.

Other foods are *thermostabilized*, which means they're treated with heat and sealed up in packaging to prevent them from spoiling—tuna fish and pudding are examples. Steak and smoked turkey are also taken up into space—they're treated with radiation to kill bacteria.

Space pudding comes in plastic cups, just like it does on Earth!

QuickBlast

Go Astro-Bananas!

Cadet, this is the moment you've been waiting for! It's space food taste-test time!

1 Grab the package of freeze-dried astro-bananas from your Space Case and tear it open like a true space traveler—that means you leave the top part of the package hanging on. If you were in space and you tore that piece completely off, it would become another piece of trash that could float away—

and it's *not* a good thing to have little bits of trash floating around your spacecraft!

2 Taste a banana. What do you think? How's the flavor? The freeze-drying process is supposed to help lock flavor in.

3 Put one banana slice in a cup of warm water and wait about ten minutes. Taste it. Is the texture like a regular banana now? Astronauts always rehydrate their dehydrated foods—they don't eat them dry!

Bathroom Break

Even the simple act of sitting on a toilet is not easy when you're weightless. Fortunately, there are restraints on the shuttle's toilet that clamp your legs down so you stay parked on the seat.

A space toilet works like a vacuum cleaner. Instead of a bowl full of water under the seat, there's a transport tube that traps solid waste. For liquid waste, there's a hose with a funnel on the end (for both men and women!). The urine is collected in a tank and emptied into space every few days—and when it gets out into space, the urine freezes into shiny crystals. Kind of gross...or beautiful (as some astronauts think!). You make the call!

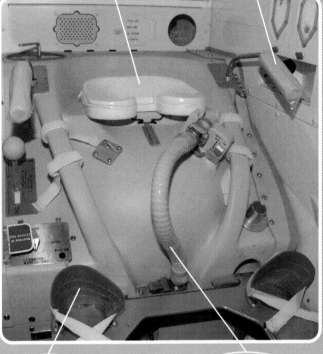

Toilet seat

Leg restraint

Foot restraint

Hose for liquid waste

Caution: If you don't strap your arms down when you sleep, they'll float out in front of you!

Sweet Dreams

At bedtime, just grab your sleeping bag and attach it with hooks to a wall or ceiling—otherwise, you'll drift through the cabin! To help you sleep, you might want to cover your eyes, use earplugs, or listen to music on headphones. It can get pretty noisy with the shuttle's fans, and with six or seven people sleeping in close quarters!

ASTRONAUT
Robert Curbeam

So, what's it like to take a space walk? To find out, Space U asked astronaut Robert L. Curbeam, Jr., who's gone on three space walks totaling over nineteen hours.

Here's Curbeam on a space walk. His job on this particular mission was to help assemble and attach a new laboratory to the International Space Station.

Question: What is it like to be outside of the space shuttle and floating in space?

Answer: It's a great feeling. The sun is so bright that you feel you're outside on a sunny day at first, but the rest of the sky is pitch black. It's funny—you have so much work that you don't think about the fact that you're doing something as incredible and enjoyable as this.

Q: On your first spacewalk, what did you find most surprising?

A: [He laughs.] We had a problem with a coolant leak. Ammonia was leaking. There was a valve that was supposed to close and it didn't. It was like being in a blizzard with all these ammonia crystals flying around. I was trying desperately to stop the leak and not damage any other hardware.

Q: How long did it take to fix?

A: About three minutes. We lost about five percent of the ammonia in the line. Everything worked out fine.

Q: Is there anything scary about spacewalks?

A: Failure is scary. There are a lot of people counting on you and you want to do your job and not let them down.

Q: What is your favorite thing about being in space?

A: The view of the Earth. This planet is absolutely beautiful. I love looking down on Earth—I could do it forever. I love taking pictures. Probably the prettiest thing I've ever seen is the Aurora Australis. We flew through it on my first mission. It's like a huge curtain of light and you see all the different colors, especially green. It's truly beautiful.

Q: What's your least favorite thing about space?

A: It's that I can't bring all my friends with me. You know how whenever you do something that's a lot of fun, you wish your friends and family could be around you? I'd like to bring a busload of my friends up to space.

This is the Aurora Australis, also called the Southern Lights. It's a display of glowing lights above the Earth caused by energized particles hitting the Earth's magnetic field. It is Robert Curbeam's favorite thing to see in space.

Part 5: Mission Control

Every NASA mission is carefully planned and monitored by a big team of "flight controllers" working in Mission Control at Johnson Space Center in Houston, Texas.

WAIT A MINUTE... DON'T SHUTTLES LAUNCH IN <u>FLORIDA</u>?

That's right—shuttles launch at Kennedy Space Center in Cape Canaveral, Florida. This is NASA's preferred launch spot for two reasons: safety and spin. It's *safer* to launch over water in case of an accident during launch, and since the Earth is *spinning* eastward, if you launch to the east, the Earth's spin will give you some extra speed. (And the closer to the equator you are, the better, because the Earth spins fastest there.) All of this makes the east coast of Florida the choice spot for launches in the United States.

This is one of the flight control teams who worked on a space shuttle mission in June 2002.

Edwards Air Force Base

Houston

Cape Canaveral

Mission Control

This is the Shuttle's alternate landing site in case the weather is bad in Florida.

And yet...Mission Control isn't in Florida, but in Houston, Texas. Blame Lyndon Johnson, as in *Johnson* Space Center, for that. When Johnson, a native Texan, was vice president in the 1960s, he said that Mission Control had to be located in Texas because he wanted his home state to be involved in the space program. So that's how we got the *Houston* in "Houston, we've had a problem here." (A phrase no flight controller wants to hear!)

FLASH FACT

The famous line, "Houston, we've had a problem here" was spoken by astronaut Jack Swigert after an explosion ripped a hole in the *Apollo 13* spacecraft in April 1970. Some say that NASA's finest hour was when its flight controllers and astronauts mustered all of their expertise and genius and found a way—against all odds—to bring the crew safely home.

WHO'S WHO IN MISSION CONTROL?

During a mission, the flight controllers work together in one big room called the Flight Control Room (FCR, pronounced "Ficker"). "Ficker" is staffed round-the-clock, but *not* by the same people—there are *three* flight control teams (each with about fifty people) per mission, and each team works for about nine hours and then hands off responsibility to the next team. The space station has its own separate mission control room. Here are just a few of the shuttle controllers:

❸ Flight Dynamics Officer (FDO, known as "Fido"): Figures out the course that the shuttle will fly to get where it needs to go, and then makes sure it *stays* on course.

❻ Flight Activities Officer (FAO): Plans the astronauts' activities and makes sure they stay on schedule.

❼ Payload Deploy and Retrieval Systems Engineer (PDRS): Monitors the shuttle's robotic arm.

❹ Flight Surgeon (SURGEON): The doctor for the crew (the word "surgeon" means the same as "doctor" here and in the military). Astronauts can have private conferences with the surgeon about health problems.

❺ Propulsion (PROP): Monitors the jets the shuttle uses to maneuver in orbit.

MISSION CONTROL CENTER

❶ Flight Director (FLIGHT): Runs the show. Leads the flight control team and is responsible for the mission.

❽ Extravehicular Activities Systems Engineer (EVA): Monitors the astronauts and their space suits during space walks.

❷ Spacecraft Communicator (CAPCOM): In charge of talking with the crew in space. The name "Capcom" comes from the old days, when astronauts flew in "capsules" instead of shuttles. The Capcom is always an astronaut, since the role requires a lot of technical knowledge that only astronauts have.

❾ Public Affairs Officer (PAO): Lets the public know what's happening on the mission.

Each flight controller sits at a console (a workstation with lots of computer displays) where they review information that comes in from the spacecraft, and they wear headsets so they can talk to each other. They're each known by their "call sign," a short form of their title (shown here in parentheses, like Capcom). When the Flight Dynamics Officer (Fido) wants to talk to the Spacecraft Communicator (Capcom), she'll begin the exchange by saying "Capcom, Fido," which means, "Capcom, this is Fido."

FLIGHT DIRECTOR
Paul Dye

To get the inside scoop on Mission Control, Space U talked with Paul Dye, NASA's Lead Flight Director of Space Shuttle Operations. Mr. Dye has worked in Mission Control on about seventy space shuttle missions—starting with the very first one in 1981! He's spent approximately 10,000 hours in Mission Control, either working on missions or training for them.

Here's Mr. Dye in the Flight Control Room during a mission.

Question: What does a flight director do?

Answer: The flight director puts together the entire package. It's a leadership role. It's my job to make sure that my troops are doing their jobs. It's kind of like conducting a symphony. I make sure the mission goes as planned, and if unexpected events happen, I make sure we take the appropriate actions.

Q: How did you learn how to do your job?

A: I've always had a fascination with flying machines. One of my first words was "airplane." When I was still in high school I became a pilot, and my college degree is in aeronautic engineering. I joined NASA right out of college. I thought that the flight director had one of the coolest jobs around. My career here has been kind of a natural progression from job to job.

Q: Why can't the astronauts handle a space shuttle mission on their own? Why is Mission Control important?

A: Space flight operations are very complex. A lot of what we do in Mission Control is support the flight crew members on orbit so they can do their jobs. We're managing systems, plotting the flight trajectory, and planning their days.

Q: What's the most fun part of your job?

A: There's so much fun that it's hard to pick any one thing. Doing something incredibly complex that most people can't do or never have done—to me, that's fun. Sitting in the control center in the middle of the night when the crew is asleep and controlling the payload bay cameras, looking at the Earth, that's fun. Looking down and seeing the Red Sea go by and then the Himalayas, and pointing the cameras up and down and seeing the steppes of Russia is very, very exciting.

QuickBlast

What's Your Call Sign?

The call sign for flight directors is "Flight" (see the previous page), but they usually choose a *personal* call sign. Paul Dye's call sign is "Iron Flight" because he's from the iron ranges (iron mining areas) of northern Minnesota. There has also been a Red Flight, a White Flight, and a Blue Flight. If you were a flight director, what would you choose for *your* personal call sign? Write it below.

My call sign: _____

Mission Control Lingo	Regular Earthling English
How do you copy?	Hello? Are you there? Can you hear me?
Roger, copy that.	Yes, got it. Understood.
Go ahead.	I'm ready and listening. Say what you have to say.
You are go.	You have official permission to begin a procedure. (This is a very serious phrase, only used when the task is very important and requires a formal go-ahead.)
We're ready. We're watching.	You don't need our official permission, but we're expecting you to begin a procedure now.

Mission Control Lingo	Regular Earthling English
Comm check.	Are our communication systems working?
Atlantis, Houston.	Space shuttle Atlantis, this is Houston calling. We'd like to speak with you.
Atlantis, Houston, in the blind, we're assuming we've lost comm...	We haven't heard a response from you, so we don't know if you can hear us, but we're going to give you some instructions anyway.
Close and lock your visors. Have a good flight.	Close your helmet's visor and get ready for liftoff! (This is the last thing that's said to the crew before launch.)

As you can see, flight controllers don't waste words! When they talk, it's quick, clear, and to the point. They don't clog up the communication lines with lots of chatter. Oh, and did you notice—they love their abbreviations. NASA is *famous* for that. Try the "QB" below to master the art of space comm!

Short and Sweet

Ops=operations
Prep=preparation
Stow=put away
Unstow=unpack
Doff=take off
Don=put on

Standby=wait
EVA= extravehicular activity
PLT=pilot
CDR=commander

QuickBlast

Talk Like a Capcom

Cadet, now it's your turn to try some NASA-speak. Translate the following phrases into Mission Control lingo:

1 You have permission to begin your extracurricular activities. Put on your backpack and go wait for the bus.

2 Hey Roy, this is Roger. Can you hear me?

3 Yes, Roger. I'm listening. Say what you have to say.

4 It's time to walk the dog. Take out the leash and prepare for cold weather conditions. (How can you abbreviate "walk the dog," and "cold weather conditions" so they're short and quick, like "EVA"?)

Check your answers on page 48...and see if you can think of *more* ways to talk like a Capcom in your daily life!

YOU MAKE THE CALL!

In Mission Control, rule #1 is: *The flight director may take any necessary action required to ensure the safety of the crew and shuttle.* The unwritten rule #2 is that you better be able to back up your decisions! Want to see what it's like to be a flight director? Then grab a seat at the console, strap on your headset, and try this!

Launch Objective

Play the role of a flight director and make some tough decisions.

Mission Procedure

1 An astronaut says he's not feeling well. You:

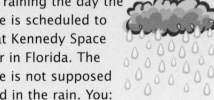

a) Ask him to describe his symptoms.

b) Arrange for the astronaut to have a private conference with the flight surgeon.

c) Direct the shuttle to come back to Earth—better to be safe than sorry!

2 The crew is out on a space walk, working with some equipment, when an important part floats away. You:

a) Have an astronaut use his backpack to fly out and get the part.

b) Maneuver the shuttle so the robotic arm can grab the part.

c) Let the part go, get the crew inside, and then move the shuttle out of the way if necessary so it won't collide with the part.

3 It's raining the day the shuttle is scheduled to land at Kennedy Space Center in Florida. The shuttle is not supposed to land in the rain. You:

a) Direct the shuttle to land at Edwards Air Force Base in California, the shuttle's alternate landing site.

b) Tell the shuttle to stay in orbit one more day to see if the weather clears up at Kennedy.

c) Land anyway! A little rain is not a big deal.

How'd You Do?

For **Question 1**, "b" is the correct choice, because you're required to respect the astronaut's privacy when it comes to medical issues. The surgeon will advise the astronaut if there's something in the shuttle's medical kit that will help him. If the situation is life-threatening, the surgeon will tell you if it's necessary to bring the shuttle back to Earth.

For **Question 2**, "c" is the right choice. It is better to lose a part than risk a crewmember not being able to get back, and moving the shuttle while the crew is outside is dangerous. The most important thing to do is make sure the crew and spacecraft are safe. Once they're secure, you can consider ways to recover or replace the part.

For **Question 3**, "b" is the best choice. It's best for the shuttle to land at Kennedy Space Center, because otherwise it has to be brought back to Florida, and that will delay the next mission that the shuttle is scheduled for. Shuttles are always supplied with enough power and food to stay in orbit up to two days after the scheduled landing day.

More from Mission Control

Trivia Quiz If the shuttle lands in California, how does it get back to Florida for its next launch? Does it get disassembled and driven back in trucks? Does it ride back on a boat? A train? A plane?

You can check your answer on page 48!

Cadet, how would you like to take a trip to the Moon...in an elevator? Or would you rather travel by flying saucer? No joke—these ideas are in the works for future space travel!

Think about how spaceflight has changed in the past fifty years—it's gone from being an idea that lots of people thought was crazy to being something we've done loads of times. Wonder what could happen in the *next* fifty years? Check out these ideas, and see if you can predict which ones will *take off....*

■ **Orbital Space Plane.** Launched on top of a rocket, this plane could ferry astronauts to and from the International Space Station, like a space taxi. The plane is designed to hold about four astronauts and a small amount of experiments and supplies for the ISS. Unlike the shuttle, the plane would not hold big payloads like satellites (which would be launched separately), and it would not have a robotic arm.

■ **Space Elevator.** Imagine a huge cable stretching from the Earth's equator all the way up into space. Then imagine boarding a vehicle that looks like a cross between a train car and spacecraft and gliding all the way up the cable into space. The cost of the trip? Super cheap! Using today's energy costs, scientists predict that the cost of a trip for one passenger with baggage would be just over $200! That's a huge bargain, considering that one space shuttle mission costs about $450 *million* dollars! To make this happen, we need to find a material strong enough to make the cable. Researchers think they've found the answer in "carbon nanotube" material, which is a hundred times stronger than steel.

■ **Hypersonic "Hyper-X" Series.** This kind of ship would take off and land just like an airplane, but it would be able to reach orbit! *Hypersonic* means that you can go more than five times the speed of sound, or more than 3,750 miles (6,035 km) per hour. That's across the entire United States in less than an hour!

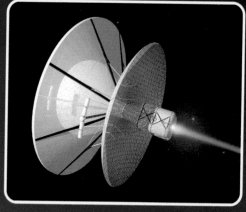

□ **Fusion Ramjet.** This spacecraft, envisioned by a physicist named Robert Bussard in 1960, is great because it doesn't have to carry any fuel! It sucks in hydrogen from space and uses *nuclear fusion* (in which hydrogen atoms are forced to join together) to create massive amounts of energy. The fusion ramjet could come close to the speed of light and travel almost anywhere in the galaxy!

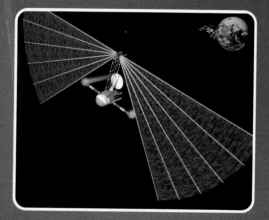

□ **Solar or Laser Sail.** Yes, we're talking about a space sailboat—sort of. Instead of wind, the sails would use light from the sun or a high-powered laser to move forward. Since it wouldn't have to carry heavy fuel, this super-light spacecraft could travel fast and far!

□ **Flying Saucer.** Fashion is a-changin', cadet— flying saucers aren't just for aliens anymore! Work is being done on the lightcraft, powered by microwaves beamed up from the ground. NASA thinks this could bring twelve people to the Moon in six hours!

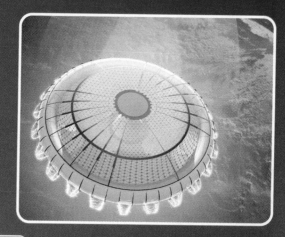

QuickBlast

Fly Me to the Future

Which of these future spacecraft ideas would *you* like to see become a reality? Cast your vote on the Space U web site at www.scholastic.com/space! (Look for the Space Travel Poll on the bulletin board.)

NEXT?

Here you are, cadet, at the end of your space travel training. And what an adventure it was! You launched rockets, orbited Earth, glided in for a landing, and now you're just about ready to touchdown....

But wait! This isn't a landing—it's really just the beginning. Now's your chance to think about the next step.

Where do *you* want to travel in space? The Moon? Mars? A grand tour of the outer solar system? Share your thoughts with other cadets in our Space Travel Poll on the Space U web site (www.scholastic.com/space). You'll find the poll on the bulletin board.

So, we'll see you next month! What'd you say, cadet? That's right: *Roger, copy that!*

THE ANSWER STATION

Page 33: You Take the Controls!

A) 8   B) 2   C) 9   D) 7   E) 1
F) 6   G) 5   H) 3

Page 44: Talk Like a Capcom
Here's how you can say each line like a Capcom. (These aren't the only right answers!)

1) You are go for ECA. Don your backpack and standby for bus pickup.

2) Roy, Roger. How do you copy?

3) Roger, Roger. Go ahead.

4) We're ready for a WD. Unstow the leash and prep for CWC.

Page 45: You Make the Call
The shuttle gets a piggy-back ride across the country from a 747 jet!

MATH TRAILBLAZERS™

Grade 3

Unit Resource Guide
Unit 11
Multiplication Patterns

SECOND EDITION

A Mathematical Journey Using Science and Language Arts

KENDALL/HUNT PUBLISHING COMPANY
4050 Westmark Drive   Dubuque, Iowa   52002

A TIMS® Curriculum
University of Illinois at Chicago

UIC The University of Illinois
at Chicago

The original edition was based on work supported by the National Science Foundation under grant No. MDR 9050226 and the University of Illinois at Chicago. Any opinions, findings, and conclusions or recommendations expressed in this publication are those of the author(s) and do not necessarily reflect the views of the granting agencies.

Printed in the United States of America

1 2 3 4 5 6 7 8 9 10   07 06 05 04 03

LETTER HOME
Multiplication Patterns

Date: _____

Dear Family Member:

In *Multiplication Patterns,* we return to the study of multiplication and division. We focus on multiplication facts. We also solve word problems involving multiplication and division to help students understand when to use each of these operations.

In third grade students become fluent with the basic multiplication facts by developing strategies for learning them. The availability of calculators does not eliminate the need to know the multiplication and division facts. We want students who can quickly estimate answers and perform calculations. For this, a knowledge of the facts is essential.

I put these 6 tiles in 2 rows of 3 tiles, so 6 = 2 × 3.

I wonder whether there are any other ways.

Exploring factors of 6

We will first work with the multiplication facts that involve 0, 1, 2, 3, 5, and 10. We call these the "Handy Facts." Next, we arrange square-inch tiles into rectangles and investigate how multiplication is related to the dimensions of the rectangles. We learn about prime numbers and square numbers. Finally, we look for patterns in the multiplication table.

Help your child by asking what he or she has learned about:

- **Square Numbers.** Ask your child to tell you why the square numbers, 1, 4, 9, 16, etc., are called "square."

- **Patterns with Nines.** Ask your child to tell you some of the patterns related to the multiplication facts for the nines.

- **Zero.** Take turns making up multiplication and division word problems involving zero.

- **Multiplication Facts.** Students will study the multiplication facts in small groups in each unit that follows. For this unit, help your child practice the multiplication facts for the fives and tens using the *Triangle Flash Cards.*

Thank you for taking the time to encourage your child's study of mathematics.

Sincerely,

_____

UNIT OUTLINE

Multiplication Patterns

Pacing Suggestions

In Lesson 4 *Completing the Table,* students assess their fluency with the multiplication facts for the fives and tens and begin a systematic review of those facts that they need to study. Work with the remaining groups of facts is distributed throughout the Daily Practice and Problems and Home Practice in each unit. All students should continue learning new concepts and skills while they are working on the facts.

Because the math facts program is closely linked to the recommended schedule for teaching lessons, classrooms that differ significantly from the suggested pacing will need to make accommodations to ensure that students receive a consistent program of math facts practice and assessment throughout the year. The *Grade 3 Facts Resource Guide* outlines a schedule for the study of the math facts in classrooms that move much more slowly through lessons than is recommended in the Lesson Guides. For more information, see the TIMS Tutor: *Math Facts* in the *Teacher Implementation Guide.*

Components Key: SG = Student Guide, DAB = Discovery Assignment Book, AB = Adventure Book, URG = Unit Resource Guide, and DPP = Daily Practice and Problems

	Sessions	Description	Supplies
LESSON 1 **Lizardland Problems** SG pages 140–144 URG pages 21–26 DPP A–B	1	**ACTIVITY:** Students solve problems involving multiplication by using clues they find in a drawing of the Lizardland Amusement Park. They then write and solve their own multiplication problems about the drawing.	• calculators
LESSON 2 **Handy Facts** DAB pages 159–164 URG pages 27–33 DPP C–D	1	**ACTIVITY:** Students generate the multiplication facts for 0, 1, 2, 3, 5, and 10; record them on a blank multiplication table; and look for patterns that arise among the table entries.	
LESSON 3 **Multiplication and Rectangles** SG pages 145–148 URG pages 34–42 DPP E–H	2	**ACTIVITY:** Students arrange square-inch tiles into rectangular arrays. They explore turn-around facts, prime numbers, and squares. They derive multiplication facts and record them on their multiplication tables.	• square-inch tiles

	Sessions	Description	Supplies

LESSON 4

Completing the Table

SG	pages 149–151		
DAB	pages 165–169		
URG	pages 43–51		
DPP	I–L		

Sessions: **2**

ACTIVITY: Students complete their multiplication tables by finding the remaining multiplication facts through skip counting or using a calculator. Symmetry in the table is discussed as well as patterns for multiples of nine. Students learn to use the *Triangle Flash Cards* to practice the multiplication facts.

Supplies:
• envelopes

LESSON 5

Floor Tiler

DAB	pages 171–173		
URG	pages 52–56		
DPP	M–N		

Sessions: **1**

GAME: After spinning two numbers, players use the product to color in rectangles on grid paper. Players take turns spinning and filling in their grids.

Supplies:
• clear plastic spinners or pencils and paper clips
• crayons or markers

LESSON 6

Division in Lizardland

SG	pages 152–154		
URG	pages 57–63		
DPP	O–P		

Sessions: **1**

ACTIVITY: Students explore the relationship between multiplication and division through problems about the Lizardland Amusement Park. They discover that there is no turn-around rule for division, and they investigate division involving zero.

LESSON 7

Cipher Force!

AB	pages 77–94		
URG	pages 64–71		
DPP	Q–R		

Sessions: **1**

ADVENTURE BOOK: A group of superheroes and their nine-year-old companion use addition, subtraction, multiplication, and division with zero to fight crime.

LESSON 8

Multiples of Tens and Hundreds

SG	page 155		
DAB	page 175		
URG	pages 72–77		
DPP	S–T		

Sessions: **1–2**

ACTIVITY: Using base-ten pieces, students investigate multiplication by multiples of 10 and 100.

Supplies:
• calculators
• base-ten pieces

CONNECTIONS

A current list of connections is available at www.mathtrailblazers.com. Detailed information on software titles can be found in Section 13 of the Teacher Implementation Guide.

Literature

Suggested Titles

- Carroll, Lewis. *Alice's Adventures in Wonderland.* Illustrated by Helen Oxenburg. 1st Candlewick Press Edition. Candlewick Press, Cambridge, MA, 1999.
- Hulme, Joy N. *Sea Squares.* Hyperion Books for Children, New York, 1993.

Software

- *Math Arena* is a collection of math activities that reinforces many math concepts.
- *Math Munchers Deluxe* provides practice with basic facts in an arcade-like game.
- *Mighty Math Calculating Crew* poses short answer questions about number operations and money skills.
- *National Library of Virtual Manipulatives* website (http://matti.usu.edu) allows students to work with manipulatives including base-ten pieces, the abacus, and many others.
- *Schoolhouse Rock: Math Rock* develops number sense and fluency with math facts.

BACKGROUND

Multiplication Patterns

In this unit, the third of four multiplication and division units in the third grade, we focus on multiplication facts. Students engage in activities that will help them develop strategies for learning the facts. We expect students to have a variety of strategies for dealing with the facts in third grade and to achieve fluency by the end of the year. This unit introduces the array model of multiplication, investigates multiplication and division with zero, and explores the patterns found when multiplying by multiples of 10 and 100.

Facts

While an understanding of concepts is our highest priority, the existence of calculators does not eliminate the need to know the multiplication and division facts. "However, calculators do not replace fluency with basic number combinations, conceptual understanding, or the ability to formulate and use efficient and accurate methods for computing." (National Council of Teachers of Mathematics, p. 145) For this, a knowledge of the facts is essential. *Math Trailblazers* takes a more conceptual approach to the learning of the basic facts and computation in general. Research has shown that fact retention is higher when facts are learned in a meaningful way. As children investigate patterns among the multiplication facts and use them in problem-solving situations and games, they will develop the ability to quickly recall them when needed.

"Fluency with the basic number combinations develops from well-understood meanings for the four operations and from a focus on thinking strategies." (National Council of Teachers of Mathematics, p. 152) Fluency with basic procedures enhances conceptual understanding of new material.

Practice

Practice is an essential part of developing fluency with the basic facts. In this unit, students are introduced to the *Triangle Flash Cards* to practice their multiplication facts. These are the same cards that will be used in fourth grade to practice division facts. By using these cards to practice the basic facts, students strengthen their understanding of multiplicative reasoning, e.g., the relationships between factors and multiples and between multiplication and division.

Arrays

In previous units, children worked with multiplication as a way to solve problems about equal groupings and jumps on the number line. In this unit, they will use arrays to represent multiplication.

An **array** is an arrangement of elements into a rectangular pattern of (horizontal) **rows** and (vertical) **columns.** For example, a candy box that contains 5 rows with 6 pieces in each row is a 5 × 6 array. One virtue of the array model is that it makes very clear the fact that 5 × 6 = 6 × 5: The box can be rotated 90 degrees to form a 6 × 5 array. Another advantage is that it creates a visual image of a multiplication problem.

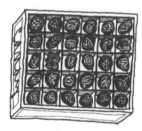 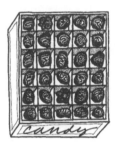

Figure 1: *From left to right, a 5 × 6 array and a 6 × 5 array*

Rate Problems

Problems involving rates occur often in the real world. Although many adults remember memorizing formulas to solve rate problems (for example, "distance = rate × time"), rate problems can be as simple as these:

- If there are 12 eggs in a dozen, how many eggs are there in three dozen?
- If we have 6 pencils in one package, how many do we have in five packages?
- If we travel 60 miles per hour, how far will we travel in 3 hours?

In the first example, the rate is the number of eggs per dozen (12); in the second example, it is the number of pencils in one package (6); and in the third, the rate is the distance we travel in 1 hour (60 miles). Students worked with a rate (8 lemons per pitcher) in the activity *Lemonade Stand* in Unit 7.

Rate problems play an important role in many of the labs in Grades 3–5. In many of these labs, students will determine the appropriate rate from a graph.

Division Involving Zero

While multiplication involving a zero factor always results in zero as the product (any number times zero is zero), there are two different cases of division involving zero.

1. Zero as a dividend. When zero is divided by any (non-zero) number, the answer is zero. For example, suppose a mother distributes all the cookies in the cookie jar equally among her three children. If there are six cookies, each child will get $6 \div 3 = 2$ cookies. Similarly, if there are zero cookies, each child will get $0 \div 3$ cookies. Children will unhappily see that $0 \div 3 = 0$.

2. Zero as a divisor. Division by zero is undefined. Here are a few ways to see why division by zero does not make sense:

   a. Division is the inverse of multiplication. Thus, to solve a problem like $45 \div 9 = N$, we ask, "What number times 9 equals 45?" Since $5 \times 9 = 45$, we know that $45 \div 9 = 5$. Similarly, to solve the problem $45 \div 0$, we would ask, "What number times 0 equals 45?" There is no such number, so it is impossible to divide 45 by zero. If we had the same discussion for another number, we would come to the same conclusion, as long as that number is itself not equal to 0. In paragraph c below, we will discuss why $0 \div 0$ is not defined.

   b. Division can also be viewed as repeated subtraction. A simple way to divide by a whole number is to repeatedly subtract that number from the dividend until zero is reached; the quotient is the number of times the divisor is subtracted. For example, to solve $15 \div 5 = N$, we can proceed as follows:

$$
\begin{array}{r}
15 \\
-\ 5 \\
\hline
10 \\
-\ 5 \\
\hline
5 \\
-\ 5 \\
\hline
0
\end{array}
$$

Since 5 was subtracted three times, we know there are three fives in 15 so that $15 \div 5 = 3$. Now, try the same thing when 0 is the divisor, as in $15 \div 0 = N$:

$$
\begin{array}{r}
15 \\
-\ 0 \\
\hline
15 \\
-\ 0 \\
\hline
15 \\
-\ 0 \\
\hline
15
\end{array}
$$

It is clear that no progress is being made. If we try to carry out a division by zero by subtracting repeatedly until nothing is left, we will be at it forever. Hence, division by zero is not possible. An example of this can be found in the Adventure Book *Cipher Force!* The silly superhero, Div, tries to fill a roller coaster with 24 Girl Scouts by putting zero scouts in the first car, zero scouts in the second car, and so on until all 24 Girl Scouts are on the roller coaster. Even an infinitely long roller coaster would not fill the bill!

   c. It is tempting to believe that $0 \div 0 = 1$. After all, $7 \div 7 = 1$, $5 \div 5 = 1$, so we could decide that $0 \div 0 = 1$. Using the definition of division in terms of multiplication, $0 \div 0 = N$ means $0 = 0 \times N$. While $N = 1$ does make this number sentence true, so would any other number. Since there is not a unique number that satisfies the condition, $0 \div 0$ is undefined.

There are other ways to see why division by zero does not make sense. All of them require examining the meaning of division.

Resources

- National Research Council. "Developing Proficiency with Whole Numbers." In *Adding It Up: Helping Children Learn Mathematics*. J. Kilpatrick, J. Swafford, and B. Findell, eds. National Academy Press, Washington, DC, 2001.
- National Research Council. "Teaching for Mathematical Proficiency." In *Adding It Up: Helping Children Learn Mathematics*. J. Kilpatrick, J. Swafford, and B. Findell, eds. National Academy Press, Washington, DC, 2001.
- *Principles and Standards for School Mathematics*. National Council of Teachers of Mathematics. Reston, VA, 2000.

Assessment Indicators

- Can students represent multiplication and division problems using arrays?
- Can students solve multiplication and division problems and explain their reasoning?
- Can students multiply numbers with ending zeros?
- Can students write number sentences for multiplication and division situations?
- Can students use patterns in the multiplication table to develop multiplication strategies?
- Can students use turn-around facts (commutativity) to multiply?
- Can students solve problems involving money?
- Do students demonstrate fluency with the multiplication facts for the 5s and 10s?

OBSERVATIONAL ASSESSMENT RECORD

(A1) Can students represent multiplication and division problems using arrays?

(A2) Can students solve multiplication and division problems and explain their reasoning?

(A3) Can students multiply numbers with ending zeros?

(A4) Can students write number sentences for multiplication and division situations?

(A5) Can students use patterns in the multiplication table to develop multiplication strategies?

(A6) Can students use turn-around facts (commutativity) to multiply?

(A7) Can students solve problems involving money?

(A8) Do students demonstrate fluency with the multiplication facts for the 5s and 10s?

(A9) _____

Name	A1	A2	A3	A4	A5	A6	A7	A8	A9	Comments
1.										
2.										
3.										
4.										
5.										
6.										
7.										
8.										
9.										
10.										
11.										
12.										
13.										

Name	A1	A2	A3	A4	A5	A6	A7	A8	A9	Comments
14.										
15.										
16.										
17.										
18.										
19.										
20.										
21.										
22.										
23.										
24.										
25.										
26.										
27.										
28.										
29.										
30.										
31.										
32.										

Daily Practice and Problems

Multiplication Patterns

Two Daily Practice and Problems (DPP) items are included for each class session listed in the Unit Outline. A Scope and Sequence Chart for the DPP can be found in the *Teacher Implementation Guide.*

A DPP Menu for Unit 11

Icons in the Teacher Notes column designate the subject matter of each DPP item. The first item in each lesson is always a Bit and the second is either a Task or Challenge. Each item falls into one or more of the categories listed below. A menu of the DPP items for Unit 11 follows.

N Number Sense C, D, F, H, I, L, Q, R, T	**✖** Computation A, E, H, I, T	**🕐** Time G, M	**⬡** Geometry N
⁵⁄ₓ₇ Math Facts B–F, J, L, N–T	**$** Money J–L, P	**⚖** Measurement	**📈** Data

Practicing and Assessing the Multiplication Facts

By the end of third grade, students are expected to demonstrate fluency with the multiplication facts. In Units 3–10, students explore multiplication patterns and develop strategies for learning the multiplication facts. In this unit, they begin the systematic, strategies-based practice and assessment of these facts. This study will take place primarily in the Daily Practice and Problems and will continue through Unit 20. The multiplication facts will be studied and assessed in groups. The sequence in which the groups will be reviewed and studied is shown in Figure 2.

Unit	Multiplication Facts
11	Practice and assess the 5s and 10s
12	Practice and assess the 2s and 3s
13	Practice and assess the square numbers
14	Practice and assess the 9s
15	Practice and assess the last six facts
16	Practice and assess the 2s, 5s, and 10s
17	Practice and assess the 3s and 9s
18	Practice and assess the square numbers
19	Practice and assess the last six facts
20	Assess all the multiplication facts groups

Figure 2: *Distribution of the multiplication facts in Units 11–20.*

Lesson 4 introduces the use of the *Triangle Flash Cards: 5s* and *10s* for studying the multiplication facts. Flash cards for each remaining group are distributed in Units 12–15 in the *Discovery Assignment Book,* immediately following the Home Practice. They can also be found in the Generic Section of the *Unit Resource Guide.* See the DPP menu above for the items that provide practice with multiplication facts. Bit S is a quiz on fives and tens.

For information on the study of the facts in Grade 3, see the Daily Practice and Problems Guide for Unit 3. For a detailed explanation of our approach to learning and assessing the math facts in Grade 3, see the *Grade 3 Facts Resource Guide* and for information for Grades K–5, see the TIMS Tutor: *Math Facts* in the *Teacher Implementation Guide.*

Daily Practice and Problems

Students may solve the items individually, in groups, or as a class. The items may also be assigned for homework.

Student Questions	Teacher Notes

A Mental Arithmetic: Adding 99

Write down these problems; then, solve them. Look for patterns.

1. 131 + 99 =   2. 555 + 99 =

3. 97 + 99 =   4. 103 + 99 =

5. 355 + 99 =   6. 769 + 99 =

7. 327 + 99 =   8. 82 + 99 =

9. 777 + 99 =

TIMS Bit

Discuss possible strategies for finding the answers to these problems. One possible strategy is to add 100 and subtract 1.

1. 230   2. 654

3. 196   4. 202

5. 454   6. 868

7. 426   8. 181

9. 876

B Multiplication Story

1. 3 × 5 = ? Write a story and draw a picture about 3 × 5. Write a number sentence on your picture.

2. 9 × 5 = ? Write a story and draw a picture about 9 × 5. Write a number sentence for your picture.

TIMS Task

1. 3 × 5 = 15

2. 9 × 5 = 45

Students may wish to share their stories with the class.

Discuss students' pictures. Ask students if they can use their pictures to solve 3 × 15.

Student Questions	Teacher Notes

C Fives and Tens

A. $5 \times 2 =$ B. $10 \times 2 =$

C. $5 \times 4 =$ D. $10 \times 4 =$

E. $5 \times 6 =$ F. $10 \times 6 =$

G. $5 \times 8 =$ H. $10 \times 8 =$

I. $5 \times 10 =$ J. $10 \times 10 =$

What patterns do you see?

TIMS Bit

A.	10	B.	20
C.	20	D.	40
E.	30	F.	60
G.	40	H.	80
I.	50	J.	100

Students may see that 10 times a number is twice 5 times that number (because 10 is twice 5). They may also see that the solutions in the first column skip count by tens and that the solutions in the second column skip count by twenty.

D Guess My Number

1. I am less than 3×4. I am greater than 2×3. I am an even number. I am not 10.

2. I am less than 4×5. I am greater than 2×7. I am 3 times some number. I am not 15.

TIMS Task

1. 8
2. 18

Student Questions	Teacher Notes

 Multiplication Facts: 0s and 1s

A. $5 \times 0 =$ B. $5 \times 1 =$

C. $10 \times 0 =$ D. $1 \times 10 =$

E. $0 \times 47 =$ F. $47 \times 1 =$

G. $0 \times 736 =$ H. $1 \times 736 =$

I. Use your calculator to check your answers.

J. What can you say about multiplying numbers by 0?

K. What can you say about multiplying numbers by 1?

TIMS Bit

After students complete these questions discuss them with the class.

A. 0   B. 5

C. 0   D. 10

E. 0   F. 47

G. 0   H. 736

J. Numbers multiplied by 0 equal 0.

K. Numbers multiplied by 1 equal themselves.

F **More Fives and Tens**

A. $5 \times 3 =$ B. $10 \times 3 =$

C. $5 \times 5 =$ D. $10 \times 5 =$

E. $5 \times 7 =$ F. $10 \times 7 =$

G. $5 \times 9 =$ H. $10 \times 9 =$

What patterns do you see?

TIMS Task

A. 15   B. 30

C. 25   D. 50

E. 35   F. 70

G. 45   H. 90

Refer to the Teacher Notes for Bit C.

G **Counting by Fives**

1. Count by 5-minute periods from 1:00 to 2:00. Make a list.

2. How many 5-minute periods are there from 1:00 to 2:00?

3. How many 5-minute periods are there in two hours?

TIMS Bit

Skip counting may help prepare students to solve problems involving elapsed time. Such problems will appear in Unit 14 Lesson 1.

1. Starting with 1:00, 1:05, 1:10, 1:15, etc.

2. 12

3. 24

Story Solving

$5 \times \frac{1}{4} = ?$ Write a story and draw a picture about $5 \times \frac{1}{4}$. Write a number sentence on your picture.

TIMS Task

$5 \times \frac{1}{4} = 1\frac{1}{4}$. Students may wish to share their stories with the class.

Lizardland Picnic

At Lizardland, eight people can sit at a table in Picnic Park. If your class had a picnic there (including your teacher), how many tables would you need? Draw a picture to show your answer.

TIMS Bit

Answers will vary according to class size.

Nickels and Dimes

You may use real or pretend money to help you solve the following problems.

1. What is the total value of 6 nickels and 4 dimes?

2. A. The total value of 55¢ is made up of 2 dimes and how many nickels?

   B. Name three other ways you can make 55¢ using only nickels and dimes.

TIMS Task

1. 70¢

2. A. 7 nickels

   B. Students should list at least 3 of the following five other ways:

   5 dimes and 1 nickel

   4 dimes and 3 nickels

   3 dimes and 5 nickels

   1 dime and 9 nickels

   0 dimes and 11 nickels

Cookies

At Max and Cora's cookie stand, one cookie costs 35¢. How many different ways can they get paid exact change for one cookie using only nickels, dimes, and quarters?

TIMS Bit $

There are 6 possibilities. A table may help students organize their work.

5¢	10¢	25¢
0	1	1
2	0	1
1	3	0
3	2	0
5	1	0
7	0	0

L **Nickels and Dimes**

True or false? Explain how you know.

1. 4 dimes < 6 nickels

2. 7 dimes and 4 nickels = 9 dimes

3. 15 nickels > 6 dimes

TIMS Task $ N

Have real or pretend money available to help students solve the problems.

1. False; 4 dimes is 40 cents, 6 nickels is 30 cents.

2. True; the 4 nickels can be exchanged for 2 dimes.

3. True; $.75 is greater than $.60.

M **Missing Time**

Copy each list below. Find the missing times.

1. 2:50, 2:55, ——, 3:05, ——, ——, 3:20

2. 4:15, 4:30, ——, ——, 5:15, ——, 5:45

3. 6:00, 5:55, ——, 5:45, ——, ——, 5:30, ——

4. 8:30, ——, 7:30, ——, 6:30, 6:00, ——

TIMS Bit

You may choose to work with a clock, showing the position of the hands for each of the times given in the problems.

Here are the missing times:

1. 3:00, 3:10, 3:15

2. 4:45, 5:00, 5:30

3. 5:50, 5:40, 5:35, 5:25

4. 8:00, 7:00, 5:30

Student Questions	Teacher Notes

 Multiplication and Rectangles

A rectangle is made from 3 rows with 8 tiles in each row.

1. Draw a picture of this rectangle on *Centimeter Grid Paper.*

2. How many tiles make up the rectangle? Write a number sentence to show your answer.

3. Make a different rectangle with the same number of tiles. How many rows? How many tiles in each row?

TIMS Task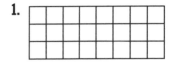

1.

2. $3 \times 8 = 24$ tiles

3. Answers will vary.

   Possible responses:
   1 row of 24 tiles;

   2 rows of 12 tiles;

   4 rows of 6 tiles;

   6 rows of 4 tiles;

   8 rows of 3 tiles;

   12 rows of 2 tiles;

   24 rows of 1 tile

 Lizardland

Use the picture of Lizardland in the *Student Guide* to help you solve the following problems.

Find the Lizardland wall at the entrance to the park.

1. How many bricks are behind the Lizardland sign? Tell how you know.

2. How many bricks are covered by the sign listing the admission prices? Tell how you know.

TIMS Bit

1. $5 \times 6 = 30$ bricks
2. $6 \times 4 = 24$ bricks

Student Questions	Teacher Notes

P **How Much and How Many?**

A. Moe spent 9 nickels and 7 dimes to buy ice cream. How much money did he spend? Show how you found your answer.

B. Joe has 5 shirts. Each shirt has 3 pockets. How many pockets are on Joe's shirts? Write a number sentence.

C. Flo has 7 braids in her hair. Each braid has 5 beads. How many beads are in Flo's hair? Write a number sentence.

TIMS Task

A. $1.15;

  9 × 5 cents = 45 cents

  7 × 10 cents = 70 cents

  45 cents + 70 cents = 115 cents

B. 3 × 5 = 15 pockets

C. 7 × 5 = 35 beads

Q **Mathhoppers**

1. A +3 mathhopper starts at 0 and hops six times. Where does it land?

2. A +5 mathhopper starts at 0 and hops eight times. Where does it land?

3. A +5 mathhopper starts at 0 and wants to eat a sunflower seed on 163. Will it be able to land on the sunflower seed? Why or why not? Think about the patterns you found in your multiplication table.

TIMS Bit

1. 18

2. 40

3. No, a +5 mathhopper lands only on numbers ending in 0 or 5. It will land on 160 and then 165. It will jump right over the sunflower seed.

R A Product of 36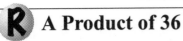

Write 36 as a product of two numbers in as many ways as you can.

TIMS Task

Have tiles and graph paper available so students can work with arrays to find the answers.

1 × 36   2 × 18   3 × 12

4 × 9   6 × 6

S Quiz on 5s and 10s

A. 5 × 2 =

B. 3 × 10 =

C. 5 × 0 =

D. 8 × 10 =

E. 6 × 10 =

F. 5 × 3 =

G. 10 × 9 =

H. 7 × 5 =

I. 10 × 2 =

J. 10 × 7 =

K. 6 × 5 =

L. 5 × 10 =

M. 8 × 5 =

N. 9 × 5 =

O. 4 × 10 =

P. 4 × 5 =

Q. 10 × 10 =

R. 5 × 5 =

TIMS Bit

This quiz is on the first group of multiplication facts, the 5s and 10s.

We recommend 2 minutes for this test. Allow students to change pens after the time is up and complete the remaining problems in a different color.

After students take the test, have them update their *Multiplication Facts I Know* charts.

Mathhopper

You may use a calculator to solve the problems. A +8 mathhopper starts at 0.

1. There is a frog at 97. Will the mathhopper land on the frog and be eaten? Tell how you know. If it does not land on the frog, how close does it get?

2. How many hops does the mathhopper need to take to get to a daisy at 224? Tell how you know.

TIMS Task

1. Discuss the patterns of the multiples of 8. Since they are even, it will not land on 97. It lands on 96; one away from the frog. If your calculator has the constant feature press: 8 + 8 = = = = etc. Each time you press =, the constant number (8) and operation (addition) are repeated.

2. 28 hops.

   With the constant feature press: 8 + 8 = = = = etc. Count the number of times you press the equal sign.

   Help students recognize that division can be used. Using the calculator, press: 224 ÷ 8 =.

   Alternately, 10 hops gets the mathhopper to 80, 20 hops to 160, 30 hops to 240. That's too far. Two hops back is 224, so the answer is 28 hops.

   Other strategies that may be used are repeated subtraction and trial and error.

LESSON GUIDE 1

Lizardland Problems

Estimated Class Sessions:
1

Students solve problems involving multiplication by using clues they find in a drawing of the Lizardland Amusement Park. They write and solve their own multiplication problems about the drawing.

Key Content

- Solving and writing problems involving multiplication.
- Communicating solutions and strategies verbally and in writing.

Daily Practice and Problems: Bit for Lesson 1

A. Mental Arithmetic: Adding 99
(URG p. 12)

Write down these problems; then, solve them. Look for patterns.

1. 131 + 99 =   2. 555 + 99 =

3. 97 + 99 =   4. 103 + 99 =

5. 355 + 99 =   6. 769 + 99 =

7. 327 + 99 =   8. 82 + 99 =

9. 777 + 99 =

DPP Task is on page 24. Suggestions for using the DPPs are on page 24.

Curriculum Sequence

Before This Unit

Students developed multiplication concepts by solving word problems in Grade 3 Unit 3 and Unit 7.

After This Unit

Students will continue to develop multiplication concepts through problem solving in Grade 3 Unit 16 Lesson 2 *Fill 'er Up,* Unit 19 *Multiplication and Division Problems,* and the Daily Practice and Problems.

Materials List

Print Materials for Students

	Math Facts and Daily Practice and Problems	Activity	Homework
Student Book — Student Guide		Lizardland Problems Pages 140–142	Lizardland Problems Homework Section Pages 142–144
Teacher Resources — Facts Resource Guide ⊙	DPP Item 11B		
Teacher Resources — Unit Resource Guide	DPP Items A–B Page 12 ⊙		

⊙ available on Teacher Resource CD

All Transparency Masters, Blackline Masters, and Assessment Blackline Masters in the Unit Resource Guide are on the Teacher Resource CD.

Supplies for Each Student

calculator

Materials for the Teacher

Observational Assessment Record (Unit Resource Guide, Pages 9–10 and Teacher Resource CD)
poster made by enlarging the Lizardland picture found on the first two *Lizardland Problems* Activity Pages
(Student Guide, Pages 140–141), optional

Before the Activity

You may wish to hang the Lizardland poster in the classroom a few days before the activity begins. Ask students to begin thinking of math questions they could ask about the poster.

Developing the Activity

Ask students to solve *Questions 1–5* on the *Lizardland Problems* Activity Pages. They will have to look carefully at the picture (on the wall or in their books) to find the information needed to answer the problems. All of the problems can be solved using multiplication; however, students should be allowed to use any methods they wish, including calculators. Encourage students to check their answers by finding solutions in different ways.

It is important for students to talk about their solution strategies. For this reason, we recommend that they work together in pairs. A whole-class discussion should follow to allow students to talk about different solution paths. Highlight the ways multiplication is used in the problems and include appropriate number sentences. Emphasize the relationship between addition number sentences and multiplication sentences.

> **TIMS Tip**
>
> Ask students to trade and solve each other's Lizardland problems.

Question 5 asks students to write their own multiplication problems. Students enjoy working with larger numbers, so their problems might involve numbers that they do not yet know how to multiply. Do not discourage students from using large numbers; problems that are too hard can be modeled with base-ten pieces or solved using calculators. Problems involving two-digit by one-digit multiplication will be dealt with in Unit 19, but many students will enjoy thinking about them now.

Student Guide - Page 140

Student Guide - Page 141

Daily Practice and Problems: Task for Lesson 1

B. Task: Multiplication Story (URG p. 12)

1. $3 \times 5 = $? Write a story and draw a picture about 3×5. Write a number sentence on your picture.

2. $9 \times 5 = $? Write a story and draw a picture about 9×5. Write a number sentence for your picture.

Suggestions for Teaching the Lesson

Math Facts

For DPP Task B students write a story and draw a picture for 9×5 and 3×5.

Homework and Practice

- Nine problems are provided for homework on the *Lizardland Problems* Activity Pages in the *Student Guide*.

- Select a few of the problems students wrote during the activity to assign for homework as well.

- Using DPP Bit A students build mental math skills by adding 99 to three-digit numbers.

To solve these problems, look for clues in the picture of Lizardland on the previous pages. Write about how you solved each problem. Use number sentences, pictures, or words.

1. Mr. Brown bought ice cream for his five children at the stand near Picnic Park. How much did he spend?

2. How many blocks are in the wall, including the blocks that are under the signs?

3. Each block in the front wall is 8 inches high.
   A. How high is the wall?
   B. Could you climb over it?
   C. Could you jump over it?
   D. Explain.

4. George has been watching the Lizard-Go-Round. It takes 30 seconds to go around one time.
   A. How many minutes does it take to go around eight times?
   B. How many times does it go around in $2\frac{1}{2}$ minutes?

5. Write a problem about Lizardland, and solve it using multiplication.

Homework

Refreshments

1. Tom is at the refreshment stand with his parents. They are buying three hot dogs, two fries, two lemonades, and one milk. How much will their order cost?

142 SG · Grade 3 · Unit 11 · Lesson 1   **Lizardland Problems**

Student Guide - Page 142

Buying Balloons

2. Mary's mother bought one balloon for Mary and one for Louise. How much did she pay?

3. José is near the Lizard Kingdom. How much did his balloons cost?

The Skyway

4. Joel wants to ride the Skyway. He is the one in line who is wearing the big hat and sunglasses. He noticed that a new car is loaded every 2 minutes. How long will he have to wait after the car that is now being loaded leaves?

The Lizard Show

5. Seats for today's Lizard Show are selling fast. So far, $400 has been collected. How many seats are left? Show your work with number sentences.

Lizardland Problems   SG · Grade 3 · Unit 11 · Lesson 1 143

Student Guide - Page 143

Assessment

Use the *Observational Assessment Record* to note students' progress solving multiplication problems and explaining solution strategies.

Leaping Lizard Roller Coaster

6. How many people can ride in all eight cars of the roller coaster at one time?

7. Jean wants to ride the roller coaster. There are 24 people in front of Jean. She is the one at the end of the line. Will there be enough room for her the next time it is loaded, or will she have to wait?

Ticket Sales

8. The Moore family—Grandmother Moore, Mr. and Mrs. Moore, and the three Moore children—is eating lunch beside Lizard Lake. It is Saturday. How much did they spend on admission tickets for the carnival? (Hint: The admission ticket price is beside the ticket taker at the front gate.)

9. How much would the Moores have saved on admission if they had come on Tuesday?

144 **SG** · Grade 3 · Unit 11 · Lesson 1   **Lizardland Problems**

Student Guide - Page 144

AT A GLANCE

Math Facts and Daily Practice and Problems

DPP Bit A builds math skills and number sense. Task B provides practice with multiplication facts.

Developing the Activity

1. Display the picture of the Lizardland Amusement Park on the *Lizardland Problems* Activity Pages in the *Student Guide.*
2. Students complete *Questions 1–5.*
3. Discuss the strategies used and the solutions found for each problem.

Homework

Assign the homework on the *Lizardland Problems* Activity Pages.

Assessment

Use the *Observational Assessment Record* to note students' abilities to solve multiplication problems and explain their reasoning.

Notes:

Student Guide

Questions 1–5 (SG p. 142)

1. $2.50

2. 150 blocks or 160 blocks; The actual wall has 15 columns of blocks. However, to allow for the space in the margins, the wall was divided. One of the columns of blocks was cut down the middle. If students do not realize this they may count 160 blocks. Accept either answer if it is properly explained.

3. **A.** 80 inches
   B. Possibly
   C. No
   D. 80 in. is almost 7 ft tall (12 in. × 84 in.)

4. **A.** 4 minutes
   B. 5 times

5. *Answers will vary. Two possible problems are: How much would it cost for 3 hamburgers and 3 milks? ($2.00 × 3) + (75¢ × 3) = $8.25

   The 2 P.M. Lizard Show sold out. If everyone leaving the show bought an ice cream bar, how much would the ice cream vendor collect? 300 × 50¢ = $150.00

Homework (SG pp. 142–144)

Questions 1–9

1. $9.25

2. $1.50

3. $4.00 (José has six balloons and 3 balloons cost $2.)

4. 8 minutes

5. 100 seats are left; $400 ÷ $2.00 = 200 seats; 300 seats − 200 seats = 100 seats

6. 32 people

7. Yes, there will be enough room for Jean.

8. $27.00; children: $9.00; adults: $18.00

9. Save $9.00; On Tuesday, the total would be $18.00; children: $4.50; adults: $13.50 Alternately, you save $1.50 for each person and 6 × $1.50 = $9.00.

*Answers and/or discussion are included in the Lesson Guide.
**Answers for all the Home Practice in the *Discovery Assignment Book* are at the end of the unit.

LESSON GUIDE

Handy Facts

Estimated Class Sessions: 1

Students generate the multiplication facts for 0, 1, 2, 3, 5, and 10; record them on a blank multiplication table; and look for patterns that arise among the table entries. The homework problems use nickels and dimes as a natural setting for practicing the facts for 5 and 10.

Key Content

- Using a multiplication table to record and retrieve multiplication facts.
- Identifying and using patterns among the multiplication facts for 0, 1, 2, 3, 5, and 10.
- Solving problems involving nickels and dimes.

Key Vocabulary

factor
multiple
product

Daily Practice and Problems: Bit for Lesson 2

C. Fives and Tens (URG p. 13)

A. $5 \times 2 =$	B. $10 \times 2 =$
C. $5 \times 4 =$	D. $10 \times 4 =$
E. $5 \times 6 =$	F. $10 \times 6 =$
G. $5 \times 8 =$	H. $10 \times 8 =$
I. $5 \times 10 =$	J. $10 \times 10 =$

What patterns do you see?

DPP Task is on page 31. Suggestions for using the DPPs are on page 31.

Materials List

Print Materials for Students

	Math Facts and Daily Practice and Problems	Activity	Homework
Student Book — Discovery Assignment Book		*My Multiplication Table* Page 159 and *Practicing Handy Facts* Page 161	*Nickels and Dimes* Pages 163–164
Teacher Resources — Facts Resource Guide	DPP Items 11C & 11D		
Teacher Resources — Unit Resource Guide	DPP Items C–D Page 13		
Teacher Resources — Generic Section		*100 Chart,* optional	

available on Teacher Resource CD

All Transparency Masters, Blackline Masters, and Assessment Blackline Masters in the Unit Resource Guide are on the Teacher Resource CD.

Supplies for Each Student

counters, number lines, or *100 Charts,* optional

Materials for the Teacher

Transparency of *My Multiplication Table* Activity Page (Discovery Assignment Book) Page 159
Observational Assessment Record (Unit Resource Guide, Pages 9–10 and Teacher Resource CD)

Developing the Activity

Tell students they will fill in the columns under the starred numbers (0, 1, 2, 3, 5, 10) on the *My Multiplication Table* Activity Page in the *Discovery Assignment Book*. These columns were chosen for this activity because these multiplication facts are easy to remember and are frequently familiar to children.

Students benefit from using concrete ways for figuring out their multiplication facts. Encourage them to use one of the following methods.

1. arranging counters or tally marks into groups
2. skip counting orally or on a *100 Chart,* number line (as a mathhopper would), or calculator

 TIMS Tip

Be sure that students save their tables since they will be needed to record more facts throughout the unit.

Begin by filling in the column under 2 together, demonstrating where the products should be written on the transparency of the *My Multiplication Table* Activity Page. Then, ask students to fill in the columns under 1, 3, 5, and 10.

The 0 column deserves a special discussion. To help students understand the zero facts, tell them two types of stories:

> For problems such as 7 × 0: *I have 7 pockets. Each pocket contains 0 pennies. How many pennies do I have in my pockets?*

> For problems such as 0 × 7: *The queen had several boxes that each contained 7 diamonds. She gave me 0 of the boxes. How many of the diamonds did she give me?*

Students will enjoy making up and sharing some stories of their own about zero. Afterwards, ask them to fill in the 0 column and the 0 row of their tables.

As students fill in each column, ask them to describe any patterns that they find. You may need to rephrase their descriptions of the patterns to help clarify their ideas. Use the terms **factor, product,** and **multiple** where appropriate. Tell them that many people use patterns to remember the facts, as seen in Figure 3.

Content Note

The Language of Multiplication. 3 × 5 = 15. We say fifteen is the **product** of three and five. We say fifteen is a **multiple** of 3 because it is the product of 3 and another whole number (namely, 5). Five and three are called **factors** of 15 (other factors of 15 are 1 and 15).

Name _____ Date _____

My Multiplication Table

Fill in the columns that are starred.

×	0	1	2	3	4	5	6	7	8	9	10
0	0										
1											
2											
3											
4											
5											
6											
7											
8											
9											
10											

In your journal, write about the patterns you see in the table. Try to find a pattern for each starred column.

Save this table. You will fill in more facts later.

Handy Facts   DAB · Grade 3 · Unit 11 · Lesson 2 159

Discovery Assignment Book - Page 159

×	0	1	2	3	4	5	6	7	8	9	10
0	0	0	0	0	0	0	0	0	0	0	0
1	0	1	2	3		5					10
2	0	2	4	6		10					20
3	0	3	6	9		15					30
4	0	4	8	12		20					40
5	0	5	10	15		25					50
6	0	6	12	18		30					60
7	0	7	14	21		35					70
8	0	8	16	24		40					80
9	0	9	18	27		45					90
10	0	10	20	30		50					100

Figure 3: *The multiplication table as filled in during this activity*

Name _____ **Date** _____

Practicing Handy Facts

Solve the following problems. Use your multiplication table when you need help.

1. $3 \times 2 =$ _____ 2. $6 \times 10 =$ _____ 3. $0 \times 10 =$ _____

4. $6 \times 5 =$ _____ 5. $8 \times 10 =$ _____ 6. $7 \times 1 =$ _____

7. $4 \times 1 =$ _____ 8. $9 \times 3 =$ _____ 9. $6 \times 2 =$ _____

10. $1 \times 4 =$ _____ 11. $9 \times 5 =$ _____ 12. $5 \times 5 =$ _____

13. $\begin{array}{r} 7 \\ \times 5 \\ \hline \end{array}$ 14. $\begin{array}{r} 7 \\ \times 2 \\ \hline \end{array}$ 15. $\begin{array}{r} 8 \\ \times 5 \\ \hline \end{array}$ 16. $\begin{array}{r} 3 \\ \times 3 \\ \hline \end{array}$

17. $\begin{array}{r} 3 \\ \times 5 \\ \hline \end{array}$ 18. $\begin{array}{r} 6 \\ \times 0 \\ \hline \end{array}$ 19. $\begin{array}{r} 0 \\ \times 2 \\ \hline \end{array}$ 20. $\begin{array}{r} 1 \\ \times 3 \\ \hline \end{array}$

21. $\begin{array}{r} 4 \\ \times 5 \\ \hline \end{array}$ 22. $\begin{array}{r} 2 \\ \times 3 \\ \hline \end{array}$ 23. $\begin{array}{r} 2 \\ \times 5 \\ \hline \end{array}$ 24. $\begin{array}{r} 5 \\ \times 2 \\ \hline \end{array}$

Write and solve a multiplication story about zero. Write a number sentence to go with it.

_____

_____

_____

_____

_____

Handy Facts   DAB · Grade 3 · Unit 11 · Lesson 2 **161**

Discovery Assignment Book - **Page 161**

Journal Prompt

Describe a pattern you find in the multiplication table. Explain why you think this pattern occurs.

PATTERNS FOR REMEMBERING THE FACTS

Patterns for 0 • All multiples of 0 are 0.

Patterns for 1 • Any number times 1 is itself.

Patterns for 2 • All multiples of 2 are even.

• All multiples of 2 are doubles.

• All multiples of 2 end in 0, 2, 4, 6, or 8.

Patterns for 5 • All multiples of 5 end in 0 or 5. When even numbers are multiplied by 5, the product ends in 0. When odd numbers are multiplied by 5, the product ends in 5.

Patterns for 10 • All multiples of 10 end in 0.

• When ten is multiplied by any number, the product is the same number with an extra 0 on the end.

Students might also observe that they get the same answer when they change the order of the factors. For example, $10 \times 3 = 3 \times 10$. This will be more apparent later when they work with a completed multiplication table.

The *Practicing Handy Facts* Activity Page in the *Discovery Assignment Book* provides practice using the table and in remembering the facts for 0, 1, 2, 3, 5, and 10. Have students complete it after they have discussed their patterns.

Suggestions for Teaching the Lesson

Math Facts

Task D provides practice with multiplication facts through number puzzles. DPP Bit C provides practice with the multiplication facts for the 5s and 10s.

Homework and Practice

The *Nickels and Dimes* Homework Pages provide practice with the multiplication facts for the fives and tens using money.

Assessment

Use the *Observational Assessment Record* to note students' abilities to use patterns to learn the multiplication facts.

Daily Practice and Problems: Task for Lesson 2

D. Task: Guess My Number

(URG p. 13)

1. I am less than 3×4. I am greater than 2×3. I am an even number. I am not 10.

2. I am less than 4×5. I am greater than 2×7. I am 3 times some number. I am not 15.

Name _____ Date _____

Nickels and Dimes

Homework

1. Complete the following table by counting money (real or pretend) or by using arithmetic.

Number of Nickels	Number of Dimes	Value of Nickels	Value of Dimes	Total Value
5	3	$.25	$.30	$.55
7	2			
	4	$.40		
	8	$.30		
2			$.90	
4			$1.00	
3			$.30	$.45
		$.05	$.50	
0	7			
9			$.10	$.55

Handy Facts

DAB · Grade 3 · Unit 11 · Lesson 2 163

Discovery Assignment Book - Page 163

Name _____ Date _____

2. How many ways can you make $.45 using only nickels and dimes? List them in the table below.

Number of Nickels	Number of Dimes	Value of Nickels	Value of Dimes	Total Value

164 DAB · Grade 3 · Unit 11 · Lesson 2

Handy Facts

Discovery Assignment Book - Page 164

AT A GLANCE

Math Facts and Daily Practice and Problems

DPP Bit C and Task D provide practice with multiplication facts.

Developing the Activity

1. Use a transparency of the *My Multiplication Table* Activity Page in the *Discovery Assignment Book* to fill in the column under 2 as a class.
2. Students fill in the columns under 1, 3, 5, and 10 using counters, tally marks, or skip counting.
3. Discuss multiplication by zero, by telling two types of stories that involve zero. Ask students to create and share similar stories and then fill in the column under 0.
4. Students discuss patterns they see in the table.
5. Students complete the *Practicing Handy Facts* Activity Page using the multiplication table.

Homework

Assign the *Nickels and Dimes* Homework Pages for homework.

Assessment

Use the *Observational Assessment Record* to note students' abilities to use patterns to learn the multiplication facts.

Notes:

Discovery Assignment Book

My Multiplication Table (DAB p. 159)

×	0	1	2	3		5					10
0	0	0	0	0		0					0
1	0	1	2	3		5					10
2	0	2	4	6		10					20
3	0	3	6	9		15					30
4	0	4	8	12		20					40
5	0	5	10	15		25					50
6	0	6	12	18		30					60
7	0	7	14	21		35					70
8	0	8	16	24		40					80
9	0	9	18	27		45					90
10	0	10	20	30		50					100

Practicing Handy Facts (DAB p. 161)

Questions 1–24

1. 6	2. 60
3. 0	4. 30
5. 80	6. 7
7. 4	8. 27
9. 12	10. 4
11. 45	12. 25
13. 35	14. 14
15. 40	16. 9
17. 15	18. 0
19. 0	20. 3
21. 20	22. 6
23. 10	24. 10

Nickels and Dimes (DAB pp. 163–164)

Questions 1–2

1.

Number of Nickels	Number of Dimes	Value of Nickels	Value of Dimes	Total Value
5	3	$.25	$.30	$.55
7	2	$.35	$.20	$.55
8	4	$.40	$.40	$.80
6	8	$.30	$.80	$1.10
2	9	$.10	$.90	$1.00
4	10	$.20	$1.00	$1.20
3	3	$.15	$.30	$.45
1	5	$.05	$.50	$.55
0	7	0	$.70	$.70
9	1	$.45	$.10	$.55

2.

Number of Nickels	Number of Dimes	Value of Nickels	Value of Dimes	Total Value
1	4	$.05	$.40	$.45
3	3	$.15	$.30	$.45
5	2	$.25	$.20	$.45
7	1	$.35	$.10	$.45

*Answers and/or discussion are included in the Lesson Guide.

**Answers for all the Home Practice in the *Discovery Assignment Book* are at the end of the unit.

E. Multiplication Facts: 0s and 1s
(URG p. 14)

A. $5 \times 0 =$ B. $5 \times 1 =$

C. $10 \times 0 =$ D. $1 \times 10 =$

E. $0 \times 47 =$ F. $47 \times 1 =$

G. $0 \times 736 =$ H. $1 \times 736 =$

I. Use your calculator to check your answers.

J. What can you say about multiplying numbers by 0?

K. What can you say about multiplying numbers by 1?

G. Counting by Fives (URG p. 14)

1. Count by 5-minute periods from 1:00 to 2:00. Make a list.

2. How many 5-minute periods are there from 1:00 to 2:00?

3. How many 5-minute periods are there in two hours?

DPP Tasks are on page 39. Suggestions for using the DPPs are on page 39.

LESSON GUIDE 3

Multiplication and Rectangles

> **Estimated Class Sessions: 2**

Students arrange square-inch tiles into rectangles to find factors of 6, 12, and 18. They turn the rectangles around and find that changing the order of the factors in a multiplication sentence does not change the product (e.g., $3 \times 6 = 18$ and $6 \times 3 = 18$). They build squares with their tiles to derive the square number multiplication facts and look for patterns among square numbers. New facts are recorded on their multiplication tables. Finally, they solve problems about tile arrangements.

Key Content

* Representing multiplication using rectangular arrays.
* Deriving turn-around facts.
* Investigating square and prime numbers.
* Solving problems involving multiplication and division.

Key Vocabulary

array
column of an array
prime number
row of an array
square number
turn-around fact

Materials List

Print Materials for Students

	Math Facts and Daily Practice and Problems	Activity	Homework
Student Book — Student Guide		*Multiplication and Rectangles* Pages 145–147	*Multiplication and Rectangles* Homework Section Page 148
Teacher Resources — Facts Resource Guide ◉	DPP Items 11E & 11F		
Unit Resource Guide	DPP Items E–H Pages 14–15 ◉		
Generic Section ◉		*Centimeter Grid Paper,* 2 per student and *Three-column Data Table,* 1 per student (optional)	*Square-Inch Grid Paper,* 1 per student

◉ *available on Teacher Resource CD*

All Transparency Masters, Blackline Masters, and Assessment Blackline Masters in the Unit Resource Guide are on the Teacher Resource CD.

Supplies for Each Student

25 square-inch tiles (of one color)

My Multiplication Table with the 0, 1, 2, 3, 5, and 10 columns completed during Lesson 2 *Handy Facts* (Discovery Assignment Book) Page 159

Materials for the Teacher

Transparency of *Centimeter Grid Paper* (Unit Resource Guide, Generic Section)

Transparency of *My Multiplication Table* with the 0, 1, 2, 3, 5, and 10 columns completed during Lesson 2 (Discovery Assignment Book) Page 159

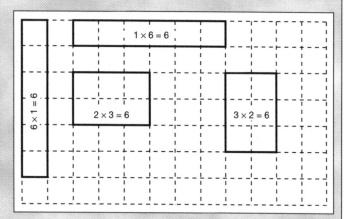

Figure 4: *Four rectangles made with six tiles*

Student Guide - Page 145

Developing the Activity

Questions 1–3 on the *Multiplication and Rectangles* Activity Pages in the *Student Guide* provide a summary for students of the steps in exploring the factors of 6 with tiles. You may prefer to lead the activity without the use of the *Student Guide*. Ask students:

• *Arrange six tiles into rectangles in as many ways as you can.*

Students should work individually and then compare their rectangles with those of a partner. Students should find four ways to arrange the six tiles, counting the arrangement of two rows and three columns, for example, as different from the arrangement of three rows and two columns. Explain that **rows** are horizontal and **columns** are vertical. Ask:

• *How many rows and columns do you see in this rectangle?*

• *Can you think of a number sentence to match this rectangle?*

After you have demonstrated this on the transparency, have students draw their rectangles on *Centimeter Grid Paper* and write multiplication sentences inside them, as in Figure 4. If students suggest number sentences using repeated addition (e.g., 2 + 2 + 2), link repeated addition with multiplication by showing how both number sentences match the rectangle. Emphasize that in this activity, students will write multiplication sentences. This procedure should be repeated for 12 and 18 tiles in *Questions 4–5.*

Exploring Factors of 6 Using Tiles

1. Arrange 6 square tiles into rectangles in as many ways as you can.

2. Draw your rectangles on *Centimeter Grid Paper*.

3. Write multiplication sentences inside each rectangle.

Exploring Factors of 12 and 18 Using Tiles

4. Arrange 12 tiles into rectangles in as many ways as you can. Then, draw your rectangles on graph paper, and write multiplication sentences inside each rectangle.

5. Do the same thing with 18 tiles.

Exploring Factors of 5 and 7 Using Tiles

6. Arrange 5 and 7 tiles into rectangles in as many ways as you can.

7. How are the rectangles you can make for 5 and 7 different from the ones you can make for 6, 12, and 18?

Exploring Turn-around Facts

8. Choose a multiplication fact, and turn its factors around. For example,

$2 \times 3 = 6$ can be turned around to make $3 \times 2 = $ _____ . Make a rectangle to match your new fact.

2 × 3 = 6

3 × 2 = 6

9. We call the facts that we get from old ones in this way **turn-around facts**. Record in your multiplication table all facts that are turn-around facts for the ones you've already recorded.

Student Guide - Page 146

In *Question 6,* students discover that the numbers 5 and 7 each have only two factors, themselves and 1. Tell them that numbers with this property are called **prime.** The only rectangles that can be made using a prime number of tiles are those with only one row or column. Ask the students to find other prime numbers by building rectangles.

In working with the tiles, students will find that multiplication is commutative—although this term is not used at this point. For *Questions 8–9,* students use the commutative property to get new facts from old by "turning around" the facts they have already found. Help students to see that a fact such as $9 \times 3 = 27$, which appears in column 3 on the *My Multiplication Table* Activity Page, is a **turn-around fact** for $3 \times 9 = 27$, which they can enter in row 3. The turn-around facts for any column in the table are in the corresponding row—for example, row 3 and column 3 have the same entries.

Exploring Square Numbers

10. Use your tiles to build squares of different sizes, up to at least 10×10. Count the number of tiles on each side and the total number of tiles in each square. Make a table like this one.

Number on a Side	Number in Square	Multiplication Facts
1	1	$1 \times 1 = 1$
2	4	$2 \times 2 = 4$
3	9	

11. The numbers 1, 4, 9, and so on are called **square numbers.** Enter your facts from Question 10 about square numbers in your multiplication table.

12. Do you see a pattern for square numbers?

Student Guide - Page 147

URG · Grade 3 · Unit 11 · Lesson 3   37

TIMS Tip

If each student has 25 tiles, he or she can build his or her own small squares, but will need to combine tiles with other students to get the 100 tiles needed to build the large squares.

For **Questions 10–12,** students build squares with their tiles to derive the squares of the numbers from 1 to 10. On a separate sheet of paper or a *Three-column Data Table* students make a table of squares similar to the one shown for **Question 10.** Then, they record the square facts on their multiplication tables. Students may notice that the square numbers run diagonally left to right through the multiplication table.

Figure 5 shows the facts they should have entered in their tables after completing **Questions 8–12.**

×	0	1	2	3	4	5	6	7	8	9	10
0	0	0	0	0	0	0	0	0	0	0	0
1	0	1	2	3	4	5	6	7	8	9	10
2	0	2	4	6	8	10	12	14	16	18	20
3	0	3	6	9	12	15	18	21	24	27	30
4	0	4	8	12	16	20					40
5	0	5	10	15	20	25	30	35	40	45	50
6	0	6	12	18		30	36				60
7	0	7	14	21		35		49			70
8	0	8	16	24		40			64		80
9	0	9	18	27		45				81	90
10	0	10	20	30	40	50	60	70	80	90	100

Figure 5: *The multiplication table as filled in during this activity*

Suggestions for Teaching the Lesson

Math Facts

DPP Bit E provides practice multiplying with 0 and 1. Task F provides practice with the multiplication facts for the fives and tens.

Homework and Practice

- Assign the Homework section in the *Student Guide*. Instead of sending tiles home, send home a sheet of *Square-Inch Grid Paper* and have the students cut it into "tiles."

- For DPP Bit G students skip count by 5-minute periods. Task H explores multiplying a fraction by a whole number.

Assessment

Homework *Questions 3–4* can be used as an assessment of students' abilities to solve problems using arrays and to write number sentences for them.

Extension

- **Prime numbers.** Ask students to use tiles in order to investigate the factors of the numbers 1 to 50 and to identify the prime numbers. You might want to assign a different set of numbers to each group so that their findings can be combined into a comprehensive class list.

- **Square numbers.** Ask students to make a list of square numbers: 0, 1, 4, 9, 16, 25, 36, 49. . . . Then, ask them to subtract consecutive square numbers and to make a list of the differences. The first few numbers in the list of differences are 1 (1 − 0), 3 (4 − 1), and 5 (9 − 4). Pose questions like these:

  1. *What pattern do you see?* (The squares go up by consecutive odd numbers.)

  2. *Does this pattern continue?* (Yes)

  3. *Can you use this pattern to predict the next square number?* (Yes, 16 = 9 + 7)

Literature Connection

- Hulme, Joy N. *Sea Squares.* Hyperion Books for Children, New York, 1993.

This book develops square number facts through counting.

Daily Practice and Problems:
Tasks for Lesson 3

F. Task: More Fives and Tens

(URG p. 14)

A. $5 \times 3 =$	B. $10 \times 3 =$
C. $5 \times 5 =$	D. $10 \times 5 =$
E. $5 \times 7 =$	F. $10 \times 7 =$
G. $5 \times 9 =$	H. $10 \times 9 =$

What patterns do you see?

H. Task: Story Solving (URG p. 15)

$5 \times \frac{1}{4} = ?$ Write a story and draw a picture about $5 \times \frac{1}{4}$. Write a number sentence on your picture.

Homework
Tile Problems

Use tiles to help you solve these problems. Write a number sentence to go with each problem.

1. Sam made a rectangle with 30 tiles. If there were 6 rows, how many were in each row?

2. Julia made a rectangle with 7 rows and 5 in each row. How many tiles did she use?

3. Sara made an array with 24 tiles. There were 8 tiles in each row. How many rows were there?

4. A rectangle of 12 tiles has tiles of 3 different colors. There is an equal number of tiles of each color. How many tiles of each color are there?

5. Arrange 20 tiles into rectangles in as many ways as you can. Write a number sentence for each rectangle.

6. Arrange 11 tiles into rectangles in as many ways as you can. Write a number sentence for each rectangle.

148 SG · Grade 3 · Unit 11 · Lesson 3   **Multiplication and Rectangles**

Student Guide - Page 148

AT A GLANCE

Math Facts and Daily Practice and Problems

DPP Bit E practices multiplication by 0 and 1. Task F is multiplication fact practice. Bit G involves time. Task H explores fraction concepts.

Developing the Activity

1. Demonstrate how rectangular arrays can represent multiplication facts.
2. Students complete *Questions 1–5* on the *Multiplication and Rectangles* Activity Pages in the *Student Guide.* They arrange tiles into rectangles and write number sentences to describe the rectangles.
3. Students answer *Questions 6–7* and learn about prime numbers.
4. For *Questions 8–9,* students learn that multiplication is commutative. They enter turn-around facts for the facts they have already found on the *My Multiplication Table* Activity Page in the *Discovery Assignment Book.*
5. For *Questions 10–12* on the *Multiplication and Rectangles* Activity Pages, students use tiles to find the squares of the numbers from 1 to 10. They make a table of squares and record the square facts on the *My Multiplication Table* Activity Page.

Homework

Assign the Tile Problems Homework section on the *Multiplication and Rectangles* Activity Pages.

Assessment

Questions 3–4 of the Homework section may be used for an assessment.

Notes:

Student Guide

Questions 1–12 (SG pp. 146–147)

1-3.* See Figure 3 in the Lesson Guide.

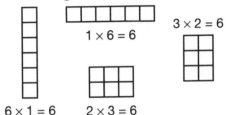

$1 \times 6 = 6$

$3 \times 2 = 6$

$6 \times 1 = 6$ $2 \times 3 = 6$

4.

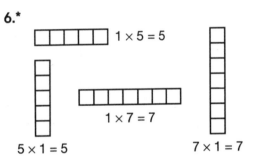

$2 \times 6 = 12$

$12 \times 1 = 12$

$4 \times 3 = 12$

$3 \times 4 = 12$

$6 \times 2 = 12$

$1 \times 12 = 12$

5.

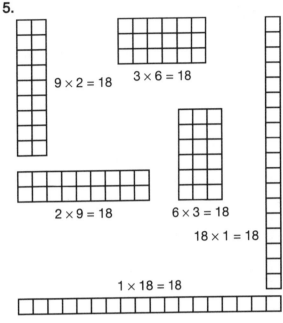

$9 \times 2 = 18$ $3 \times 6 = 18$

$2 \times 9 = 18$ $6 \times 3 = 18$

$18 \times 1 = 18$

$1 \times 18 = 18$

6.*

$1 \times 5 = 5$

$1 \times 7 = 7$

$5 \times 1 = 5$ $7 \times 1 = 7$

7. Using 5 or 7 tiles you can make only two rectangles. When using 6, 12, or 18 tiles, you can form 4 or 6 different rectangles.

8.* Answers will vary.

9.* At this time, in addition to the starred columns, the following rows should be completed on the *My Multiplication Table* Activity Page in the *Discovery Assignment Book:* 0s, 1s, 2s, 3s, 5s, and 10s.

*Answers and/or discussion are included in the Lesson Guide.

**Answers for all the Home Practice in the *Discovery Assignment Book* are at the end of the unit.

10.

Number on a Side	Number in Square	Multiplication Facts
1	1	$1 \times 1 = 1$
2	4	$2 \times 2 = 4$
3	9	$3 \times 3 = 9$
4	16	$4 \times 4 = 16$
5	25	$5 \times 5 = 25$
6	36	$6 \times 6 = 36$
7	49	$7 \times 7 = 49$
8	64	$8 \times 8 = 64$
9	81	$9 \times 9 = 81$
10	100	$10 \times 10 = 100$

Homework (SG p. 148)

Questions 1–6

Number sentences may vary.

1. 5 tiles; $6 \times 5 = 30$ tiles
2. 35 tiles; $7 \times 5 = 35$ tiles
3. 3 rows; $24 \div 8 = 3$ rows
4. 4 tiles; $12 \div 3 = 4$ tiles
5. $1 \times 20 = 20$, $20 \times 1 = 20$, $2 \times 10 = 20$, $10 \times 2 = 20$, $4 \times 5 = 20$, $5 \times 4 = 20$
6. $11 \times 1 = 11$, $1 \times 11 = 11$

11.* See Figure 5 in the Lesson Guide. The facts from the table above should be added to the *My Multiplication Table* Activity Page in the *Discovery Assignment Book.*

12. Answers will vary. The difference between the squares goes up by consecutive odd numbers. The square numbers run diagonally upper left to lower right through the multiplication table.
   *See the Extension section in the Lesson Guide.

*Answers and/or discussion are included in the Lesson Guide.
**Answers for all the Home Practice in the *Discovery Assignment Book* are at the end of the unit.

LESSON GUIDE

Completing the Table

Estimated Class Sessions:
2

In Part 1, students complete their multiplication tables by finding the remaining multiplication facts through skip counting or using a calculator. Symmetry in the table is discussed as well as patterns for multiples of 9. In Part 2, students learn how to use the *Triangle Flash Cards: 5s* and *10s* to practice the facts. They begin their *Multiplication Facts I Know* charts.

Key Content

* Identifying patterns for multiples of nine.
* Investigating symmetry in the multiplication table.

Key Vocabulary

symmetry

Daily Practice and Problems: Bits for Lesson 4

I. Lizardland Picnic (URG p. 15)

At Lizardland, eight people can sit at a table in Picnic Park. If your class had a picnic there (including your teacher), how many tables would you need? Draw a picture to show your answer.

K. Cookies (URG p. 16)

At Max and Cora's cookie stand, one cookie costs 35¢. How many different ways can they get paid exact change for one cookie using only nickels, dimes, and quarters?

DPP Tasks are on page 48. Suggestions for using the DPPs are on page 48.

Curriculum Sequence

Before This Unit

In Units 2–10, students reviewed and were assessed on the subtraction facts primarily through the Daily Practice and Problems. They also developed strategies for the multiplication facts.

After This Unit

In Units 12–20, students will continue to practice and assess the multiplication facts. In each unit, they will study a small group of facts in the Daily Practice and Problems. In Grade 4 students will review the multiplication facts and develop fluency with the division facts.

Materials List

Print Materials for Students

	Math Facts and Daily Practice and Problems	Activity	Homework
Student Books			
Student Guide		*Completing the Table* Pages 149–151	*Completing the Table* Homework Section Page 151
Discovery Assignment Book		*Triangle Flash Cards: 5s* Page 165, *Triangle Flash Cards: 10s* Page 167, and *Multiplication Facts I Know* Page 169	Home Practice Parts 1 & 2 Page 156
Teacher Resources			
Facts Resource Guide 💿	DPP Items 11J & 11L Use *Triangle Flash Cards: 5s* and *Triangle Flash Cards: 10s* to practice the multiplication facts for these groups.		
Unit Resource Guide	DPP Items I–L Pages 15–16 💿		
Generic Section 💿		*Small Multiplication Tables,* 2 small tables per student, 1 for class and 1 for home, (optional)	

💿 *available on Teacher Resource CD*

All Transparency Masters, Blackline Masters, and Assessment Blackline Masters in the Unit Resource Guide are on the Teacher Resource CD.

Supplies for Each Student

calculator, optional
My Multiplication Table, partially completed in Lessons 2 and 3 (Discovery Assignment Book) Page 159
envelope for storing flash cards

Materials for the Teacher

Transparency of *My Multiplication Table,* partially completed in Lessons 2 and 3 (Discovery Assignment Book) Page 159
Multiplication Table Transparency Master (Unit Resource Guide) Page 50

Developing the Activity

Part 1. Patterns for Nine

The *Completing the Table* Activity Pages in the *Student Guide* begin by pointing out to students that they only need to find a few more facts to complete their multiplication tables. Remind them that when they find a fact, such as 4 × 6, they can also record its turn-around fact, 6 × 4. When students begin the lesson, they should have 20 blank squares left (from the original 121) in their multiplication tables. Because of the turn-around rule of multiplication, they actually have only 10 facts remaining.

Have students figure out the remaining facts in any manner they wish. Some good strategies include using skip counting, a calculator, a number line, or counters. Another good strategy is to use known facts to derive the new ones. For example, a student might add to the known fact 5 × 4 = 20 to derive the new fact 6 × 4 = 24:

"I know that 5 × 4 = 20. So, 6 × 4 is 4 more—24." A student might subtract from the known fact 5 × 8 = 40 to derive the new fact 4 × 8 = 32: "I know that 5 × 8 is 40. So, 4 × 8 is 8 less—32."

After completing their multiplication tables, students look for patterns in their tables. They have already looked for patterns in earlier activities, but will probably see new ones in the completed table.

Question 1 asks students to look for patterns with nines. In discovering patterns in *Question 2,* students might observe the following:

1. When the products are listed in a column, as below, it is easy to see that the digits in the ten's place count up by ones (0, 1, 2, 3 . . .) and that the digits in the one's place count down by ones (9, 8, 7 . . .).

    9
    18
    27
    36
    45
    54
    63
    72
    81

Completing the Table

You should have only 20 blank squares left in your multiplication table. Use any strategy you like—skip counting, a calculator, a number line, or counters—to find the remaining facts.

When you find a fact, such as 4 × 6, you can also record its turn-around fact—in this case, 6 × 4.

Patterns for Nine

1. Copy and complete the list of facts for 9. Then, write the products in a column, one on each line.

   0 × 9 = ?

   1 × 9 = ?

   2 × 9 = ?

   3 × 9 = ?

   4 × 9 = ?

   5 × 9 = ?

   6 × 9 = ?

   7 × 9 = ?

   8 × 9 = ?

   9 × 9 = ?

2. What patterns do you see in your list?

Completing the Table   SG · Grade 3 · Unit 11 · Lesson 4   149

Student Guide - Page 149

TIMS Tip

It often helps in remembering nine's facts to see how simple it is to derive them from the familiar ten's facts. For example, "10 × 4 is 40. So, 9 × 4 is 4 less: 40 − 4 = 36" and "10 × 5 is 50. So, 9 × 5 is 5 less: 50 − 5 = 45."

3. Use your calculator to find the products below. Then, add the digits in each product. Repeat adding the digits until you get a one digit number.

Example: $9 \times 634 = 5706$ $5 + 7 + 0 + 6 = 18$ $1 + 8 = 9$

A. 9×47 B. 9×83

C. 9×89 D. 9×92

E. 9×123 F. 9×633

G. 9×697 H. 9×333

4. Describe what happens when you add the digits of a multiple of 9.

Multiplication Facts and Triangle Flash Cards

With a partner, use the directions below and your Triangle Flash Cards: 5s and Triangle Flash Cards: 10s to practice the multiplication facts.

- One partner covers the shaded number, the largest number on the card. This number will be the answer to the multiplication problem. It is called the **product.**

- The second person multiplies the two uncovered numbers (one in a circle, one in a square). These are the two **factors.** It doesn't matter which of the factors is said first. 4×5 and 5×4 both equal 20.

$5 \times 4 = ?$

$4 \times 5 = ?$

- Separate the facts into three piles: those facts you know and can answer quickly, those that you can figure out with a strategy, and those that you need to learn.

150   SG · Grade 3 · Unit 11 · Lesson 4   **Completing the Table**

Student Guide - Page 150

Name _____ Date _____

Multiplication Facts I Know

- Circle the facts you know well.
- Keep this table and use it to help you multiply.
- As you learn more facts, you may circle them too.

×	0	1	2	3	4	5	6	7	8	9	10
0	0	0	0	0	0	0	0	0	0	0	0
1	0	1	2	3	4	5	6	7	8	9	10
2	0	2	4	6	8	10	12	14	16	18	20
3	0	3	6	9	12	15	18	21	24	27	30
4	0	4	8	12	16	20	24	28	32	36	40
5	0	5	10	15	20	25	30	35	40	45	50
6	0	6	12	18	24	30	36	42	48	54	60
7	0	7	14	21	28	35	42	49	56	63	70
8	0	8	16	24	32	40	48	56	64	72	80
9	0	9	18	27	36	45	54	63	72	81	90
10	0	10	20	30	40	50	60	70	80	90	100

Completing the Table   DAB · Grade 3 · Unit 11 · Lesson 4   169

Discovery Assignment Book - Page 169

---

2. The sums of the two digits in each of the products listed is nine. For example, $3 + 6 = 9$ and $7 + 2 = 9$. In fact, the sum of the digits of any multiple of 9 is also a multiple of 9. Furthermore, the process of adding digits can be repeated until nine itself results. As illustrated in **Question 3,** $9 \times 634 = 5706$. Adding the product's digits provides a multiple of nine: $5 + 7 + 0 + 6 = 18$. Adding the new answer's digits results in nine: $1 + 8 = 9$. In **Question 3,** students work with other multiples of nine to discover that this pattern is consistent.

Students may notice other patterns in their multiplication tables. They may notice that the diagonal line from the top left corner to the bottom right corner is a line of symmetry formed by the square numbers. To see this, students can circle a number above the line and connect it to its matching number on the bottom half, as in Figure 6.

×	0	1	2	3	4	5	6	7	8	9	10
0	0	0	0	0	0	0	0	0	0	0	0
1	0	1	2	3	4	5	6	7	8	9	10
2	0	2	4	6	8	10	12	14	16	18	20
3	0	3	6	9	12	15	18	21	24	27	30
4	0	4	8	12	16	20	24	28	32	36	40
5	0	5	10	15	20	25	30	35	40	45	50
6	0	6	12	18	24	30	36	42	48	54	60
7	0	7	14	21	28	35	42	49	56	63	70
8	0	8	16	24	32	40	48	56	64	72	80
9	0	9	18	27	36	45	54	63	72	81	90
10	0	10	20	30	40	50	60	70	80	90	100

Figure 6: *Symmetry in the multiplication table*

TIMS Tip

Adding the digits of the product of a nine's fact to see whether they add up to nine can be a strategy for remembering nine's facts. For example, a student might think, "Let me see, does 9×6 equal 54 or 56? It must be 54 since $5 + 4$ is 9, but $5 + 6$ is not 9."

Journal Prompt

Describe the patterns in your multiplication table.

Part 2. Multiplication Facts and Triangle Flash Cards

The *Triangle Flash Cards: 5s* and *Triangle Flash Cards: 10s* are located in the *Discovery Assignment Book.* The *Student Guide* outlines how students use the *Triangle Flash Cards* for practicing the multiplication facts. Partners cover the number that is shaded (the largest number on the card). This is the **product,** the answer to the multiplication problem that the other two numbers, the **factors,** present. The student being quizzed multiplies the two numbers that are showing, gives the answer, and the answer is checked.

As their partners quiz them on the facts, students sort the cards into three piles—those facts they can answer quickly, those facts they know using a strategy, and those facts they need to learn. Then each student begins a *Multiplication Facts I Know* chart found in the *Discovery Assignment Book.* Students circle those facts they know and can answer quickly on the chart. Remind students that if they know a fact, they also know its turn-around fact. So if they circle 5 × 3 = 15, they can also circle 3 × 5 = 15.

Review with students what they have learned about multiplication by zero and one in Lesson 2. Students can also circle these facts.

Students make a list of the facts they did not circle on their charts. They take this list home along with their flash cards so they can practice the facts they need to study with a family member. Students will take a quiz on the multiplication facts for the fives and tens in DPP Bit S at the end of this unit. After the quiz, they update their charts.

As students encounter multiplication problems with the facts in the activities and labs, encourage them to share their strategies. The fives and tens are easily solved using skip counting. For descriptions of other multiplication facts strategies, see the TIMS Tutor: *Math Facts* in the *Teacher Implementation Guide.*

Instruct students to keep their *Multiplication Facts I Know* charts in a safe place. They will use the charts to track their own progress learning the multiplication facts as they continue to study the facts in Units 12–20.

TIMS Tip

Use the *Small Multiplication Tables* Generic Page to make a small multiplication table for each student. (There are four tables on each page.) Students can tape them to their desks or notebooks for easy reference so they have ready access to all the facts while they are working on activities or playing games.

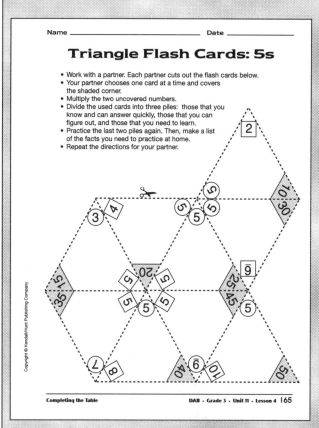

Discovery Assignment Book - Page 165

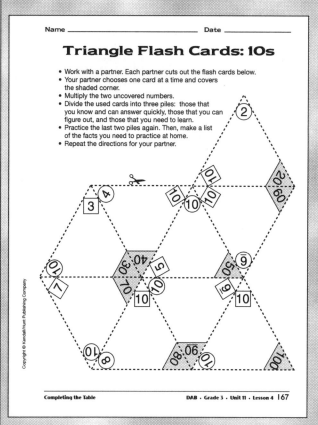

Discovery Assignment Book - Page 167

Daily Practice and Problems:
Tasks for Lesson 4

J. Task: Nickels and Dimes

(URG p. 15)

You may use real or pretend money to help you solve the following problems.

1. What is the total value of 6 nickels and 4 dimes?

2. A. The total value of 55¢ is made up of 2 dimes and how many nickels?

3. B. Name three other ways you can make 55¢ using only nickels and dimes.

L. Task: Nickels and Dimes

(URG p. 16)

True or false? Explain how you know.

1. 4 dimes < 6 nickels

2. 7 dimes and 4 nickels = 9 dimes

3. 15 nickels > 6 dimes

Suggestions for Teaching the Lesson

Math Facts

DPP items J and L provide practice with the multiplication facts for the fives and tens using problems with nickels and dimes.

Homework and Practice

- Assign the Homework section in the *Student Guide.* Allow students to take home their completed multiplication tables.

- DPP Bit I builds number sense through a division word problem. Bit K is a problem involving money.

- Remind students to practice the multiplication facts for the fives and tens throughout the rest of this unit using their *Triangle Flash Cards.*

- Parts 1 and 2 of the Home Practice can be assigned for homework. They provide addition and subtraction practice.

Answers for Parts 1 and 2 of the Home Practice can be found in the Answer Key at the end of this lesson and at the end of this unit.

- Discuss how you can figure out facts that you do not recall right away. Share your strategies with your partner.

- Practice the last two piles again and then make a list of the facts you need to practice at home for homework.

- Circle the facts you know quickly on your *Multiplication Facts I Know* chart. Remember that if you know one fact, you also know its turn-around fact. Circle both on your chart.

Multiplication Facts I Know										
×	0	1	2	3	4	5	6	7	8	9	10
0	0	0	0	0	0	0	0	0	0	0	0
1	0	1	2	3	4	5	6	7	8	9	10
2	0	2	4	6	8	10	12	14	16	18	20
3	0	3	6	9	12	15	18	21	24	27	30
4	0	4	8	12	16	20	24	28	32	36	40
5	0	5	10	15	20	25	30	35	40	45	50
6	0	6	12	18	24	30	36	42	48	54	60
7	0	7	14	21	28	35	42	49	56	63	70
8	0	8	16	24	32	40	48	56	64	72	80
9	0	9	18	27	36	45	54	63	72	81	90
10	0	10	20	30	40	50	60	70	80	90	100

Homework

Find these products.

1. $3 \times 4 = ?$
2. $6 \times 7 = ?$
3. $6 \times 5 = ?$
4. $5 \times 4 = ?$
5. $7 \times 9 = ?$
6. $4 \times 2 = ?$
7. $8 \times 5 = ?$
8. $8 \times 8 = ?$
9. $7 \times 4 = ?$
10. $0 \times 6 = ?$
11. $7 \times 3 = ?$
12. $9 \times 6 = ?$
13. $6 \times 8 = ?$
14. $7 \times 8 = ?$
15. $9 \times 9 = ?$

16. $\begin{array}{r} 7 \\ \times 5 \\ \hline \end{array}$
17. $\begin{array}{r} 6 \\ \times 9 \\ \hline \end{array}$
18. $\begin{array}{r} 3 \\ \times 8 \\ \hline \end{array}$

19. $\begin{array}{r} 4 \\ \times 6 \\ \hline \end{array}$
20. $\begin{array}{r} 8 \\ \times 3 \\ \hline \end{array}$
21. $\begin{array}{r} 9 \\ \times 1 \\ \hline \end{array}$

22. $\begin{array}{r} 8 \\ \times 4 \\ \hline \end{array}$
23. $\begin{array}{r} 6 \\ \times 6 \\ \hline \end{array}$
24. $\begin{array}{r} 7 \\ \times 7 \\ \hline \end{array}$

25. Choose one of the facts in Questions 1–24, and write a multiplication story about it. Draw a picture to go with your story.

Completing the Table

SG · Grade 3 · Unit 11 · Lesson 4 **151**

Student Guide - Page 151

Name _____ Date _____

Unit 11: Home Practice

Part 1

1. $160 - 70 =$ _____
2. $120 - 50 =$ _____
3. $140 - 60 =$ _____
4. $82 +$ _____ $= 100$
5. $53 +$ _____ $= 100$
6. $44 +$ _____ $= 100$

7. When Tony cleaned his mom's car he found some coins under the seats. His mom let him keep the coins and gave him \$.25 more for cleaning the car. Now he has \$2.00.

   A. How much money did Tony find in the car? _____

   B. What coins and how many of each could he have found? Give two possible answers.

Part 2

1. $600 + 700 =$ _____
2. $400 + 800 =$ _____
3. $500 + 900 =$ _____
4. $1000 -$ _____ $= 450$
5. $1000 -$ _____ $= 343$

6. Tina's high school graduating class has 321 students. Rita's junior high graduating class has 132 students. Sara, who is graduating from kindergarten, is in a class of 42 students.

   A. How many more students are in Tina's class than in Rita's?

   B. If all three classes attend the same ceremony, how many students would be graduating there?

156 DAB · Grade 3 · Unit 11   MULTIPLICATION PATTERNS

Discovery Assignment Book - Page 156

AT A GLANCE

Math Facts and Daily Practice and Problems

Bits I and K are word problems. DPP items J and L provide practice with multiplication facts.

Part 1. Patterns for Nines

1. Using any method they choose, students fill in ten of the blank spaces on *My Multiplication Table* for Lessons 2 and 3.
2. Students use turn-around facts to fill in the remaining blank spaces.
3. Students look for patterns with multiples of nine and discuss using the patterns to learn the facts.
4. Students look for symmetry in their multiplication tables. Use the *Multiplication Table* Transparency Master to model the symmetry of the table.
5. Students complete **Questions 1–4** of the *Completing the Table* Activity Pages in the *Student Guide.*

Part 2. Multiplication Facts and Triangle Flash Cards

1. Following the directions in the *Student Guide*, students practice the facts for the fives and tens using *Triangle Flash Cards.*
2. Students sort their cards into three piles according to how well they know each fact. They begin their *Multiplication Facts I Know* charts by circling the facts they know well and can answer quickly.
3. Students make a list of the fives and tens that they still need to learn.
4. Students review multiplication by zero and one and circle these facts on their charts.

Homework

1. Assign the Homework section of the *Completing the Table* Activity Pages.
2. Students take home their lists of facts they need to study and the *Triangle Flash Cards* in order to practice the facts with a family member.
3. Assign Parts 1 and 2 of the Home Practice.

Notes:

Multiplication Table

×	0	1	2	3	4	5	6	7	8	9	10
0	0	0	0	0	0	0	0	0	0	0	0
1	0	1	2	3	4	5	6	7	8	9	10
2	0	2	4	6	8	10	12	14	16	18	20
3	0	3	6	9	12	15	18	21	24	27	30
4	0	4	8	12	16	20	24	28	32	36	40
5	0	5	10	15	20	25	30	35	40	45	50
6	0	6	12	18	24	30	36	42	48	54	60
7	0	7	14	21	28	35	42	49	56	63	70
8	0	8	16	24	32	40	48	56	64	72	80
9	0	9	18	27	36	45	54	63	72	81	90
10	0	10	20	30	40	50	60	70	80	90	100

Student Guide

Questions 1–4 (SG pp. 149–150)

1. 0, 9, 18, 27, 36, 45, 54, 63, 72, 81
2.* Answers will vary.
3. **A.*** 423; $4 + 2 + 3 = 9$
   B.* 747; $7 + 4 + 7 = 18$
   C. 801; $8 + 0 + 1 = 9$
   D. 828; $8 + 2 + 8 = 18$
   E. 1107; $1 + 1 + 0 + 7 = 9$
   F. 5697; $5 + 6 + 9 + 7 = 27$
   G. 6273; $6 + 2 + 7 + 3 = 18$
   H. 2997; $2 + 9 + 9 + 7 = 27$
4. The sum is a multiple of 9.

Homework (SG p. 151)

Questions 1–25

1. 12	2. 42
3. 30	4. 20
5. 63	6. 8
5. 40	8. 64
9. 28	10. 0
11. 21	12. 54
13. 48	14. 56
15. 81	16. 35
17. 54	18. 24
19. 24	20. 24
21. 9	22. 32
23. 36	24. 49

25. Answers will vary.

Discovery Assignment Book

**Home Practice (DAB p. 156)

Part 1

Questions 1–7

1. 90
2. 70
3. 80
4. 18
5. 47
6. 56
7. **A.** $1.75
   B. Answers will vary. Examples: 7 quarters or 1 quarter, 5 dimes, and 20 nickels

Part 2

Questions 1–6

1. 1300
2. 1200
3. 1400
4. 550
5. 657
6. **A.** 189 students
   B. 495 students

---

*Answers and/or discussion are included in the Lesson Guide.

**Answers for all the Home Practice in the *Discovery Assignment Book* are at the end of the unit.

LESSON GUIDE 5

Floor Tiler

Estimated Class Sessions: 1

After spinning two numbers, a player uses their product to color in grid squares in the shape of a rectangle on his or her grid paper. Players take turns spinning and filling in their grids.

Key Content

- Practicing multiplication facts.
- Using the array model of multiplication to learn the multiplication facts.

Materials List

Print Materials for Students

	Math Facts and Daily Practice and Problems	Game
Student Book — Discovery Assignment Book		*Floor Tiler* Pages 171–172 and *Spinners 1–4 and 1–10* Page 173
Teacher Resources — Facts Resource Guide ⊙	DPP Item 11N	
Teacher Resources — Unit Resource Guide	DPP Items M–N Pages 16–17 ⊙	
Teacher Resources — Generic Section ⊙		*Centimeter Grid Paper,* 1 per student

⊙ *available on Teacher Resource CD*

All Transparency Masters, Blackline Masters, and Assessment Blackline Masters in the Unit Resource Guide are on the Teacher Resource CD.

Supplies for Each Student

crayon or marker

Supplies for Each Student Pair

clear plastic spinner or pencil and paper clip

Materials for the Teacher

Transparency of *Centimeter Grid Paper* (Unit Resource Guide, Generic Section), optional
Transparency of *Spinners 1–4 and 1–10* (Discovery Assignment Book) Page 173, optional
Observational Assessment Record (Unit Resource Guide, Pages 9–10 and Teacher Resource CD)

Discovery Assignment Book - Page 171

Name _____ Date _____

Floor Tiler

This game can be played by two to four players.

Materials

- $\frac{1}{2}$ sheet of *Centimeter Grid Paper* per player
- *Spinner 1–4*
- *Spinner 1–10*
- A crayon or marker for each player

Rules

1. The first player makes two spins so that he or she has two numbers. The player may either spin one spinner twice or spin each spinner once.

Floor Tiler   DAB · Grade 3 · Unit 11 · Lesson 5   171

Discovery Assignment Book - Page 172

Name _____ Date _____

2. The player must then find the **product** of the two numbers he or she spun. For example, $3 \times 4 =$ **12**.

3. After finding the product, the player colors in a rectangle that has the same number of grid squares on the grid paper. For example, he or she might color in 3 rows of 4 squares for a total of 12 squares. But the player could have colored in 2 rows of 6 squares or 1 row of 12 squares instead. (Remember, the squares colored in must connect so that they form a rectangle.)

4. Once the player has made his or her rectangle, the player draws an outline around it and writes its number sentence inside. For example, a player who colored in 3 rows of 4 squares would write "$3 \times 4 = 12$." A player who colored in 2 rows of 6 squares would write "$2 \times 6 = 12$."

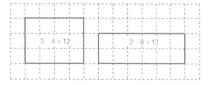

5. Players take turns spinning and filling in their grids.

6. If a player is unable to fill in a rectangle for his or her spin, he or she loses the turn, and the next player can play.

7. The first player to fill in his or her grid paper completely wins the game.

8. If no player is able to color in a rectangle in three rounds of spinning, the player with the fewest squares of the grid left is the winner.

172 DAB · Grade 3 · Unit 11 · Lesson 5   Floor Tiler

Before the Activity

Each student will need one-half sheet of *Centimeter Grid Paper*. You can instruct the pairs to cut the grid in half or have the sheets cut ahead of time.

Developing the Game

This game is for 2–4 players. The rules for playing *Floor Tiler* are found on the *Floor Tiler* Game Pages in the *Discovery Assignment Book*. A student spins to find two numbers for a multiplication sentence. He or she may use either two spins from one spinner or one spin from each spinner. After finding the product, the player colors in a rectangle with that number of squares, outlining this rectangle and recording its number sentence inside. Players continue in this fashion until one player fills in his or her grid completely. You may want to demonstrate the game using a transparency of *Centimeter Grid Paper* while a volunteer spins the spinners.

A good strategy is to use two spins from *Spinner 1–10* at the beginning of the game and two spins from *Spinner 1–4* near the end of the game. This way, the player gets to fill in large rectangles when his or her grid is empty and small rectangles when space gets tight. Encourage students to try a variety of strategies.

It will become difficult to fill in the grid completely when only a few squares are left. Rule #8 deals with this situation. If no player is able to color in a rectangle in three rounds of spinning, the player with the fewest squares left is the winner. This rule is helpful if students find the end of the game too slow moving.

Suggestions for Teaching the Lesson

Math Facts

DPP Task N provides practice with multiplication facts using rectangular arrays.

Homework and Practice

- Students can take home the Game Pages and grid paper and use pencil-and-paper-clip spinners to play at home. They record the number of minutes they play with family members or friends.

- DPP Bit M asks students to skip count to measure time by various intervals.

Assessment

Use the *Observational Assessment Record* to assess students' abilities to represent multiplication using rectangular arrays.

Extension

You can also play this game as a class by using transparencies of the spinners. Each student will fill in a rectangle on his or her half-sheet of *Centimeter Grid Paper*. Since players will fill in the grid differently, they will finish at different times. The first to finish is the winner.

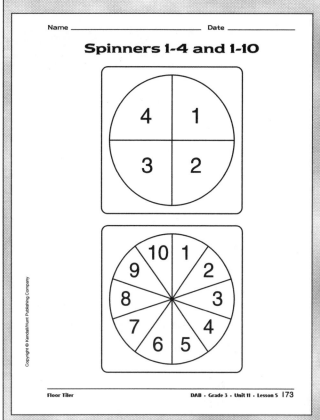

Discovery Assignment Book - Page 173

Daily Practice and Problems: Task for Lesson 5

N. Task: Multiplication and Rectangles (URG p. 17)

A rectangle is made from 3 rows with 8 tiles in each row.

1. Draw a picture of this rectangle on *Centimeter Grid Paper.*

2. How many tiles make up the rectangle? Write a number sentence to show your answer.

3. Make a different rectangle with the same number of tiles. How many rows? How many tiles in each row?

AT A GLANCE

Math Facts and Daily Practice and Problems

DPP Bit M provides practice with time and Task N provides practice with multiplication facts.

Developing the Game

1. Students read the rules on the *Floor Tiler* Game Pages in the *Discovery Assignment Book.*
2. Students play *Floor Tiler* in groups of 2–4.

Homework

Students play *Floor Tiler* at home.

Assessment

Use the *Observational Assessment Record* to note students' abilities to represent multiplication using rectangular arrays.

Notes:

LESSON GUIDE 6

Division in Lizardland

Students explore the relationship between multiplication and division through problems about the Lizardland Amusement Park. They discover that there is no turn-around rule for division, they investigate division involving zero, and they look at the relationship between multiplication and division.

Key Content

* Solving problems involving division.
* Investigating division involving zero.
* Investigating whether there is a turn-around rule for division.
* Writing number sentences for division situations.

Daily Practice and Problems: Bit for Lesson 6

0. Lizardland (URG p. 17)

Use the picture of Lizardland in the *Student Guide* to help you solve the following problems.

Find the Lizardland wall at the entrance to the park.

1. How many bricks are behind the Lizardland sign? Tell how you know.

2. How many bricks are covered by the sign listing the admission prices? Tell how you know.

DPP Task is on page 60. Suggestions for using the DPPs are on page 60.

Curriculum Sequence

Before This Unit

Students explored concepts of division in Unit 7 Lesson 4 *Birthday Party* and Lesson 5 *The Money Jar*.

After This Unit

Students will revisit division in Unit 19.

Materials List

Print Materials for Students

	Math Facts and Daily Practice and Problems	Activity	Homework
Student Books			
Student Guide		*Division in Lizardland* Pages 152–153	*Divison in Lizardland* Homework Section Page 154
Discovery Assignment Book			Home Practice Parts 3 & 4 Page 157
Teacher Resources			
Facts Resource Guide	DPP Items 11*O* & 11P		
Unit Resource Guide	DPP Items O–P Pages 17–18		

available on Teacher Resource CD

All Transparency Masters, Blackline Masters, and Assessment Blackline Masters in the Unit Resource Guide are on the Teacher Resource CD.

Supplies for Each Student

counters, optional

My Multiplication Table, completed in previous lessons (Discovery Assignment Book) Page 159

Materials for the Teacher

Classroom copy of Lizardland poster from Lesson 1, optional

Developing the Activity

Students begin by completing *Questions 1–7* from *Division in Lizardland* Activity Pages in the *Student Guide*. To find the information needed to solve the problems, they refer to the picture of Lizardland in Lesson 1 of the *Student Guide*.

Each of these problems can be solved using division. Some students may use the related multiplication facts or repeated subtraction, and some students will need to model the problems with counters or pictures. Encourage students to use the multiplication facts they have been working with to obtain the related division facts. As students share how they derived their answers, write number sentences on the board and discuss the relationship between multiplication and division. Point out that a problem such as 21 ÷ 7 can be solved by thinking:

- *How many 7s are there in 21?* or
- *What number times 7 equals 21?*

Multiplication facts and their related division facts are often referred to as **fact families.** Students might want to use their completed copy of *My Multiplication Table*.

Questions 4 and *5* provide an opportunity to discuss whether there is a turn-around rule for division. In *Question 4,* Mrs. Moore has three oranges to share among six people: $3 \div 6 = \frac{1}{2}$. Drawing a picture can help students solve this problem. In *Question 5,* Mrs. Moore shares six cookies among her three children: $6 \div 3 = 2$. Use these examples to point out that changing the order of the terms in a division sentence, unlike a multiplication sentence, does change the answer. *There is no turn-around rule for division.*

Questions 6 and *7* provide an opportunity to discuss division involving zero. In *Question 6,* Mr. Moore has zero cupcakes to share among six people. Each person receives zero cupcakes, so $0 \div 6 = 0$. In fact, *0 divided by any non-zero number is 0.* In *Question 7,* the ticket taker has 100 game tokens to distribute to the families as they enter the park. Students examine what will happen if he distributes different numbers of tokens to the families. Depending on how many he gives to each family, he runs out after different numbers: Giving 4 game tokens to each family, he runs out after 25 families enter; giving 2 tokens, 50 families; giving 1 token, 100 families. These situations can be represented by these division sentences: $100 \div 4 = 25$, $100 \div 2 = 50$, and $100 \div 1 = 100$. If, however, he gives 0 game tokens to each family as they enter, then more and more families will enter the park, but he will never run out of tokens. Therefore, there is no numerical value for

---

Division in Lizardland

Look at the picture of Lizardland to help you solve the following problems. Write number sentences to show the answers.

The Brownies

1. There are 21 Brownies and 3 leaders near Picnic Park. To make sure no one gets lost, the leaders split the troop into three smaller groups, each with its own adult leader. Each group is the same size. How many Brownies are in each group?

2. The 21 Brownies and their 3 leaders rode the Leaping Lizard Roller Coaster. How many cars on the roller coaster did they fill?

3. Each table in Picnic Park can seat eight people. Are there enough empty tables for the Brownies and their leaders?

The Moore Family

4. The Moore family is having a picnic by Lizard Lake. Mrs. Moore brought three large oranges to be shared among her family of six. How much will each person get? Write a division sentence for your answer.

5. Mrs. Moore brought six cookies to be shared among her 3 children. How many cookies will each child get? Write a division sentence for your answer. Compare your number sentence with the one you got for Question 4.

152 SG · Grade 3 · Unit 11 · Lesson 6   Division in Lizardland

Student Guide - Page 152

Zero

6. Mr. Moore baked some cupcakes for his family to share. Unfortunately, he didn't remember to bring them, so he had zero cupcakes to share among six people. Use this story to write about the value of 0 ÷ 6.

7. The ticket taker has 100 game tokens to give to the first several families who enter the park.
   A. If he gives 4 game tokens to each family that enters the park, how many families will get four tokens before he runs out? If he gives 2 game tokens to each family, how many families will get a token if he gives 1 token to each family? Be sure to write number sentences to show your answers.
   B. If he gives 0 tokens to each family, how many families will enter the park before he runs out of tokens? Use this story to tell about the value of 100 ÷ 0.

Fact Families

Multiplication and division facts are related. Questions 8–10 will show you what they have in common. The four facts in each question make up a **fact family.**

8. A. 4 × 5 = ?
   B. 5 × 4 = ?
   C. 20 ÷ 5 = ?
   D. 20 ÷ 4 = ?

9. A. 2 × 9 = ?
   B. 9 × 2 = ?
   C. 18 ÷ 2 = ?
   D. 18 ÷ 9 = ?

10. A. 6 × 8 = ?
    B. 8 × 6 = ?
    C. 48 ÷ 8 = ?
    D. 48 ÷ 6 = ?

Division Symbols

The symbols in these division sentences mean the same thing:

$$24 \div 6 = 4 \qquad 24/6 = 4 \qquad 6\overline{)24} = 4$$

11. 16/4 = ?

12. 45 ÷ 9 = ?

13. $8\overline{)64}$

14. $5\overline{)40}$

Division in Lizardland   SG · Grade 3 · Unit 11 · Lesson 6   153

Student Guide - Page 153

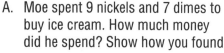
Homework

Related Multiplication and Division Problems

1. A. $8 \times 3 = ?$
   B. $24 \div 3 = ?$
   C. $24/8 = ?$
   D. $3 \times 8 = ?$

2. A. $6 \times 4 = ?$
   B. $24/4 = ?$
   C. $24 \div 6 = ?$
   D. $4 \times 6 = ?$

3. A. $5 \times 8 = ?$
   B. $40 \div 8 = ?$
   C. $5\overline{)40}$
   D. $8 \times 5 = ?$

4. A. $9 \times 6 = ?$
   B. $54 \div 6 = ?$
   C. $9\overline{)54}$
   D. $6 \times 9 = ?$

Division Problems

5. $8 \div 2 = ?$
6. $27/3 = ?$
7. $10/1 = ?$
8. $6\overline{)36}$
9. $40 \div 10 = ?$
10. $72/9 = ?$
11. $18/3 = ?$
12. $0 \div 7 = ?$
13. $25 \div 5 = ?$
14. $60/6 = ?$
15. $4\overline{)12}$
16. $3\overline{)21}$

17. Write a division story that fits one of the number sentences in Questions 1–16.

Daily Practice and Problems: Task for Lesson 6

P. Task: How Much and How Many? (URG p. 18) $\boxed{\$}$ $\boxed{\begin{smallmatrix}5\\\times 7\end{smallmatrix}}$

A. Moe spent 9 nickels and 7 dimes to buy ice cream. How much money did he spend? Show how you found your answer.

B. Joe has 5 shirts. Each shirt has 3 pockets. How many pockets are on Joe's shirts? Write a number sentence.

C. Flo has 7 braids in her hair. Each braid has 5 beads. How many beads are in Flo's hair? Write a number sentence.

$100 \div 0$. We say that *division by 0 is undefined*. (See the Background for a discussion of division by zero.)

Questions 8–10 show students number sentences for related fact families. These problems can be done aloud as a group, individually on paper, or with a partner.

Questions 11–14 are division problems similar to those in the homework problems. Point out to students that they will see three different symbols for division: $24 \div 6$, $\frac{24}{6}$, and $6\overline{)24}$. As you write division sentences on the board, vary the notation so students will become familiar with all three.

Suggestions for Teaching the Lesson

Math Facts

DPP Bit O practices multiplication facts using rectangular arrays in the Lizardland picture. Task P provides practice with the multiplication facts for the 5s and 10s in word problems.

Homework and Practice

*   Assign the problems in the Homework section of the *Division in Lizardland* Activity Pages in the *Student Guide.* Have students take home completed multiplication tables for this work.
*   Parts 3 and 4 of the Home Practice can be assigned for homework.

Answers for Parts 3 and 4 of the Home Practice can be found in the Answer Key at the end of this lesson and at the end of this unit.

Assessment

Students can write an answer for homework ***Question 17*** in class as an assessment of their understanding of division.

Literature Connection

At this point, students will have learned that, unlike the commutative multiplication sentences, order is very important in division sentences. They might enjoy hearing the following excerpt from *Alice in Wonderland,* in which the Mad Hatter points out several other places where order is important.

> The Hatter opened his eyes very wide on hearing this; but all he *said* was, "Why is a raven like a writing-desk?"
>
> "Come, we shall have some fun now!" thought Alice. "I'm glad they've begun asking riddles—I believe I can guess that," she added aloud.
>
> "Do you mean that you think you can find out the answer to it?" said the March Hare.
>
> "Exactly so," said Alice.
>
> "Then you should say what you mean," the March Hare went on.
>
> "I do," Alice hastily replied; "at least—at least I mean what I say—that's the same thing, you know."
>
> "Not the same thing a bit!" said the Hatter. "Why, you might just as well say that 'I see what I eat' is the same thing as 'I eat what I see!' "
>
> "You might just as well say," added the March Hare, "that 'I like what I get' is the same thing as 'I get what I like!' "
>
> "You might just as well say," added the Dormouse, which seemed to be talking in its sleep, "that 'I breathe when I sleep' is the same thing as 'I sleep when I breathe!' "
>
> "It *is* the same thing with you," said the Hatter, and here the conversation dropped, and the party sat silent for a minute, while Alice thought over all she could remember about ravens and writing-desks, which wasn't much.

- Carroll, Lewis. *Alice's Adventures in Wonderland.* Illustrated by Helen Oxenbury. 1st Candlewick Press Edition. Candlewick Press, Cambridge, MA, 1999.

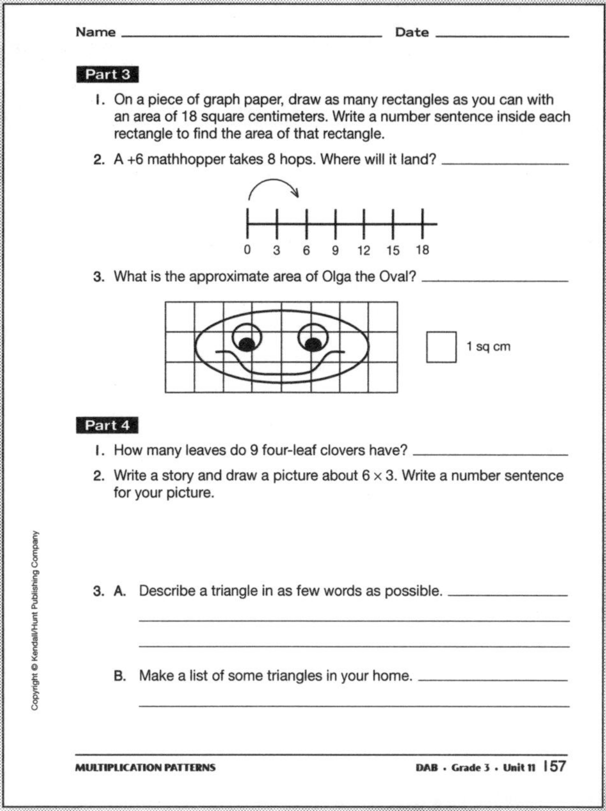

Name ______________________ Date ______________

Part 3

1. On a piece of graph paper, draw as many rectangles as you can with an area of 18 square centimeters. Write a number sentence inside each rectangle to find the area of that rectangle.
2. A +6 mathhopper takes 8 hops. Where will it land? ______________

0 3 6 9 12 15 18

3. What is the approximate area of Olga the Oval? ______________

1 sq cm

Part 4

1. How many leaves do 9 four-leaf clovers have? ______________
2. Write a story and draw a picture about 6 × 3. Write a number sentence for your picture.
3. A. Describe a triangle in as few words as possible. ______________

   B. Make a list of some triangles in your home. ______________

Copyright © Kendall/Hunt Publishing Company

MULTIPLICATION PATTERNS DAB • Grade 3 • Unit 11 157

***Discovery Assignment Book* - Page 157**

AT A GLANCE

Math Facts and Daily Practice and Problems

DPP items O and P practice multiplication facts.

Developing the Activity

1. Students complete *Questions 1–5* from the *Division in Lizardland* Activity Pages in the *Student Guide* using the Lizardland picture as a reference.
2. Students share how each problem was solved and compare number sentences to look at the relationship between multiplication and division.
3. Students complete *Questions 6–7* and discuss division involving zero.
4. Students complete *Questions 8–10* on fact families.
5. Students complete *Questions 11–14* using three different symbols for division.

Homework

1. Assign the Homework section of the *Division in Lizardland* Activity Pages.
2. Assign Parts 3 and 4 of the Home Practice.

Assessment

Question 17 of the Homework section can be used as an assessment.

Notes:

Student Guide

Questions 1–14 (SG pp. 152–153)

*Number sentences will vary.

1. 7 Brownies; $21 \div 3 = 7$ Brownies
2. 6 cars; $24 \div 4 = 6$ cars
3. Yes; $8 \times 3 = 24$
4.* $\frac{1}{2}$ orange; $3 \div 6 = \frac{1}{2}$ orange
5.* 2 cookies; $6 \div 3 = 2$ cookies
6.* Since there are no cupcakes, each person will get 0 cupcakes.
7. A.*$100 \div 4 = 25$ families;
   $100 \div 2 = 50$ families;
   $100 \div 1 = 100$ families

   B. No answer; He will never run out of tokens. An endless amount of people could enter and he would still have the 100 tokens. So $100 \div 0$ does not make sense (it is not defined).

8. A. 20
   B. 20
   C. 4
   D. 5

9. A. 18
   B. 18
   C. 9
   D. 2

10. A. 48
    B. 48
    C. 6
    D. 8

11. 4
12. 5
13. 8
14. 2

Homework (SG p. 154)

Questions 1–17

1. A. 24
   B. 8
   C. 3
   D. 24

2. A. 24
   B. 6
   C. 4
   D. 24

3. A. 40
   B. 5
   C. 8
   D. 40

4. A. 54
   B. 9
   C. 6
   D. 54

5. 4
6. 9
7. 10
8. 6
9. 4
10. 8
11. 6
12. 0
13. 5
14. 10
15. 3
16. 7
17. Answers will vary.

Discovery Assignment Book

**Home Practice (DAB p. 157)

Part 3

Questions 1–3

1. Combinations for rectangle dimensions:
   1 cm by 18 cm rectangle or 18 cm by 1 cm;
   2 cm by 9 cm rectangle or 9 cm by 2 cm;
   3 cm by 6 cm rectangle or 6 cm by 3 cm rectangle
2. 48
3. 10–12 sq cm

Part 4

Questions 1–3

1. 36 leaves
2. Answers will vary. $6 \times 3 = 18$.
3. A. Answers will vary. A 3-sided closed figure with 3 angles. The 3 sides come together at 3 corners.
   B. Answers will vary.

*Answers and/or discussion are included in the Lesson Guide.
**Answers for all the Home Practice in the *Discovery Assignment Book* are at the end of the unit.

Daily Practice and Problems:
Bit for Lesson 7

Q. Mathhoppers (URG p. 18)

1. A +3 mathhopper starts at 0 and hops six times. Where does it land?

2. A +5 mathhopper starts at 0 and hops eight times. Where does it land?

3. A +5 mathhopper starts at 0 and wants to eat a sunflower seed on 163. Will it be able to land on the sunflower seed? Why or why not? Think about the patterns you found in your multiplication table.

DPP Task is on page 71. Suggestions for using the DPPs are on page 71.

LESSON GUIDE **7**

Cipher Force!

Estimated Class Sessions: 1

The Cipher Force is a team of four superheroes and their sidekick. The superheroes—Multiply by Zero, Divide by Zero, Add Zero, and Subtract Zero—embody basic operations with zero. Several silly adventures show what happens when these operations with zero are used.

Key Content

- Identifying and using patterns in addition, subtraction, and multiplication with zero.
- Understanding why division by zero is impossible.

Key Vocabulary

cipher
null

Materials List

Print Materials for Students

	Math Facts and Daily Practice and Problems	Activity	Written Assessment
Student Book — Adventure Book		*Cipher Force!* Pages 77–94	
Teacher Resources — Facts Resource Guide	DPP Items 11Q & 11R		DPP Item 11R *A Product of 36*
Teacher Resources — Unit Resource Guide	DPP Items Q–R Pages 18–19		DPP Item R *A Product of 36* Page 19

available on Teacher Resource CD

All Transparency Masters, Blackline Masters, and Assessment Blackline Masters in the Unit Resource Guide are on the Teacher Resource CD.

Before the Activity

In the story, the superhero Divide by Zero attempts to carry out two divisions by zero. Once, he designs a roller coaster with room for zero passengers in each car; another time, he invents a 0 Mathhopper. To make these episodes more accessible, discuss similar problems that do not involve zero before you read the story. For example, ask:

- *How many roller coaster cars are required for 24 Girl Scouts if each car can carry 4 girls?*

Link this problem with the number sentence $24 \div 4 = N$ and with a solution using repeated subtraction. The story puts 24 Girl Scouts on a silly roller coaster where each car carries 0 girls. This is linked to the number sentence $24 \div 0 = N$. It is "solved" using repeated subtraction.

You can also discuss how many hops various Mathhoppers need to hop to get from 0 to 100. The number sentence $100 \div 5 = N$ can be linked to the question:

- *How many hops does a +5 Mathhopper need to travel from 0 to 100?*

The story asks how many hops it would take a +0 Mathhopper to travel from 0 to 100. The number sentence that represents this question is $100 \div 0 = N$. See the Background in this unit for a further discussion of division by zero.

TIMS Tip

You may want to read the story twice: once to get the plot and again to draw out more of the mathematics.

Adventure Book - Page 78

Page 78

- *What does* cipher *mean?*

Our word **cipher** comes from the Arabic word *sifr* meaning empty (as in an empty column on a counting board or abacus). *Zero* comes from the same root. Many mathematical terms derive from the Arabic language (e.g., *algebra, algorithm*) because of the work of medieval Arabic mathematicians.

- *Why is the Cipher Force's hideout called Null House?*

Null is another word for zero.

Adventure Book - Page 79

Page 79

- *What does the Cipher Force insignia ($\emptyset$) stand for?*

The empty set; nothing.

Page 80

- *How would you explain to Mult why any number times zero is zero?*

One possibility: No matter how many sets or groups of zero you have, you still have zero.

Adventure Book - Page 80

Page 81

- *What's wrong with Div's "zero coaster" idea?*

There is no true answer—he would never have enough cars.

- *What does Div's design have to do with dividing by zero?*

Division can be accomplished by repeatedly subtracting the divisor to make groups. See the *Background* for further discussion.

- *Show how Conrad could use his method to find how many baskets on a Ferris Wheel are needed if 15 people want to ride and each basket holds 3 people. What number sentence could go with this situation?*

$15 - 3 - 3 - 3 - 3 - 3 = 0$. Three was subtracted five times, so five baskets are needed. $15 \div 3 = 5$. Try more problems with different divisors and dividends; link each problem situation to a division sentence.

Adventure Book - Page 81

Adventure Book - Page 82

Adventure Book - Page 85

Page 82

- *Which of the two sets of kids look more alike, Multiply by Zero and Divide by Zero or Add Zero and Subtract Zero?*

Add Zero and Subtract Zero are identical twins.

- *Which hero is wearing a cape?*

Multiply by Zero is wearing a cape.

- *Why do you suppose Add Zero and Subtract Zero look so much alike?*

Because adding and subtracting by zero yield the same result: the original number.

Page 85

- *Add Zero and Subtract Zero say they are completely different. Is that true?*

No, not only do they look quite similar, but their properties—addition with zero and subtraction with zero—always yield the same results: the original number.

- *Who else took from the rich and gave to the poor?*

Robin Hood and Zorro.

- *What happens when Subtract Zero takes nothing from the rich?*

Nothing. The rich still have the same amount of money.

- *What does this have to do with subtracting zero?*

They have exactly what they had before—this is the effect of subtracting zero.

Discussion Prompts

Page 87

- *What happens when Add Zero gives nothing to the poor?*

Nothing.

- *What does this have to do with adding zero?*

They have exactly what they had before—this is the effect of adding zero.

Adventure Book - Page 87

Page 90

- *Is Conrad speaking real English?*

Yes and no. Some of these words are made up, and some have to do with space travel or computers.

- *How do you think Cipher Force will fight the aliens?*

Answers will vary. Ask students to think about what each character usually does.

Adventure Book - Page 90

Adventure Book - Page 91

Discussion Prompts

Page 91

- *What will happen when Subtract Zero takes nothing from the aliens?*

Nothing.

- *What is a number sentence that might go with this?*

Aliens − 0 = Aliens

Adventure Book - Page 92

Page 92

- *What will happen when Add Zero adds nothing to her forces?*

Nothing.

- *What is a number sentence that might go with this?*

Forces + 0 = Forces

- *What does Div mean when he says "I'll finish them off none by none"?*

We usually say one by one (meaning one at a time). He will divide by using repeated subtraction; he'll subtract zero at a time.

- *Who defeats the aliens? Why?*

Mult does because multiplying anything by zero results in nothing (zero). She made nothing out of the aliens.

Discussion Prompts

Page 94

- *Write a division problem for Div's new Mathhopper. Can you solve your problem?*

Example: How many hops does it take a 0 Mathhopper to get to 24? There is no answer to such a problem; it will never reach 24.

 Journal Prompt

- Write an adventure for Zero the Digit, the new member of the Cipher Force. Tell how Zero the Digit plays an important role in writing numbers.

- Write about what happens when (1) you add zero to any number, (2) you subtract zero from any number, (3) you multiply any number by zero, and (4) you divide any number by zero.

- Explain to Div why his 0 Mathhopper won't ever get to 100.

- Who is the strongest member of the Cipher Force? Explain why his or her powers are the best.

Suggestions for Teaching the Lesson

Math Facts

DPP Bit Q provides practice with multiplication facts using mathhoppers.

Homework and Practice

Remind students to practice at home for the quiz on the multiplication facts using the *Triangle Flash Cards: 5s* and *10s*.

Assessment

- To assess this lesson, students can write a response to one of the first three Journal Prompts.

- DPP item R can be used to assess students' abilities to write number sentences for multiplication situations.

Adventure Book - Page 94

Daily Practice and Problems: Task for Lesson 7

R. Task: A Product of 36 (URG p. 19)

Write 36 as a product of two numbers in as many ways as you can.

S. Quiz on 5s and 10s (URG p. 19)

A. $5 \times 2 =$

B. $3 \times 10 =$

C. $5 \times 0 =$

D. $8 \times 10 =$

E. $6 \times 10 =$

F. $5 \times 3 =$

G. $10 \times 9 =$

H. $7 \times 5 =$

I. $10 \times 2 =$

J. $10 \times 7 =$

K. $6 \times 5 =$

L. $5 \times 10 =$

M. $8 \times 5 =$

N. $9 \times 5 =$

O. $4 \times 10 =$

P. $4 \times 5 =$

Q. $10 \times 10 =$

R. $5 \times 5 =$

DPP Task is on page 75. Suggestions for using the DPPs are on page 75.

LESSON GUIDE 8

Multiples of Tens and Hundreds

Using base-ten pieces, students investigate multiplication by multiples of 10 and 100.

Key Content

- Multiplying by tens and hundreds.
- Communicating patterns found when multiplying by tens and hundreds.

Materials List

Print Materials for Students

	Math Facts and Daily Practice and Problems	Activity	Homework	Written Assessment
Student Guide		*Multiples of Tens and Hundreds* Page 155		
Discovery Assignment Book			*Professor Peabody's Multiplication Tables* Page 175	
Facts Resource Guide	DPP Items 11S & 11T			DPP Item 11S *Quiz on 5s and 10s*
Unit Resource Guide	DPP Items S–T Pages 19–20			DPP Item S *Quiz on 5s and 10s* Page 19

(Student Books) — Student Guide, Discovery Assignment Book

(Teacher Resources) — Facts Resource Guide, Unit Resource Guide

available on Teacher Resource CD

All Transparency Masters, Blackline Masters, and Assessment Blackline Masters in the Unit Resource Guide are on the Teacher Resource CD.

Supplies for Each Student

calculator
set of base-ten pieces
My Multiplication Table, completed in previous activities (Discovery Assignment Book) Page 159

Materials for the Teacher

Transparency of *Professor Peabody's Multiplication Tables* (Discovery Assignment Book) Page 175
Observational Assessment Record (Unit Resource Guide, Pages 9–10 and Teacher Resource CD)
Individual Assessment Record Sheet (Teacher Implementation Guide, Assessment section and
    Teacher Resource CD)
overhead base-ten pieces, optional

Multiples of Tens and Hundreds

1. What pattern for multiplying a number by ten did you find in the multiplication table? Write two examples that show your pattern.

2. Use the pattern to predict these products. Use a calculator to check your predictions.
   - A. $10 \times 24 = ?$
   - B. $10 \times 37 = ?$
   - C. $10 \times 40 = ?$
   - D. $10 \times 348 = ?$
   - E. $100 \times 6 = ?$
   - F. $100 \times 12 = ?$
   - G. $100 \times 34 = ?$
   - H. $100 \times 876 = ?$

3. Solve the following problems.
   - A. $2 \times 3 = ?$
   - B. $2 \times 30 = ?$
   - C. $2 \times 300 = ?$
   - D. $2 \times 4 = ?$
   - E. $2 \times 40 = ?$
   - F. $2 \times 400 = ?$
   - G. $3 \times 6 = ?$
   - H. $3 \times 60 = ?$
   - I. $3 \times 600 = ?$
   - J. $4 \times 3 = ?$
   - K. $4 \times 30 = ?$
   - L. $4 \times 300 = ?$

4. Solve the following problems.
   - A. $\begin{array}{r} 200 \\ \times 5 \\ \hline \end{array}$
   - B. $\begin{array}{r} 300 \\ \times 3 \\ \hline \end{array}$
   - C. $\begin{array}{r} 600 \\ \times 4 \\ \hline \end{array}$
   - D. $\begin{array}{r} 500 \\ \times 7 \\ \hline \end{array}$
   - E. $\begin{array}{r} 900 \\ \times 5 \\ \hline \end{array}$
   - F. $\begin{array}{r} 600 \\ \times 5 \\ \hline \end{array}$

Student Guide - Page 155

Developing the Activity

In **Question 1** on the *Multiples of Tens and Hundreds* Activity Page in the *Student Guide,* students recall the pattern they found in their multiplication tables for multiplying a number by ten: Write a zero at the end of the number. In **Question 2,** they use this pattern to predict the result of multiplying two- and three-digit numbers by ten. Then, they use their calculators to verify that the pattern of attaching a zero still holds.

> **Journal Prompt**
>
> Describe patterns for multiplying a number by 10, by 100, and by multiples of 10 and 100.

Questions 3–4 involve multiplying by tens and hundreds. Work on an example of this type together before students work on their own. Write "3 × 50" on the board and ask students to tell you the product and to describe how they solved the problem. Some might use repeated addition, and some might use the related fact $3 \times 5 = 15$. Model the problem using base-ten pieces, as shown in Figure 7. Show three groups of five skinnies. Students can count skinnies by tens to find that $3 \times 50 = 150$. Encourage them to use the base-ten pieces to solve the remaining problems.

Figure 7: *Modeling 3 × 50 with base-ten pieces*

Suggestions for Teaching the Lesson

Math Facts

DPP Task T builds number sense and fluency with multiplication facts using mathhopper questions.

Homework and Practice

More practice with multiplying by tens is provided on the *Professor Peabody's Multiplication Tables* Homework Page in the *Discovery Assignment Book*.

Assessment

* DPP Bit S is a quiz on the 5s and 10s and assesses multiplication facts. Use the *Observational Assessment Record* to note students' fluency with the multiplication facts for the fives and tens.

* Transfer appropriate documentation from the Unit 11 *Observational Assessment Record* to students' *Individual Assessment Record Sheets*.

Daily Practice and Problems: Task for Lesson 8

T. Task: Mathhopper (URG p. 20)

You may use a calculator to solve the problems. A +8 mathhopper starts at 0.

1. There is a frog at 97. Will the mathhopper land on the frog and be eaten? Tell how you know. If it does not land on the frog, how close does it get?

2. How many hops does the mathhopper need to take to get to a daisy at 224? Tell how you know.

Name _____ Date _____

Professor Peabody's Multiplication Tables

Homework

Professor Peabody started to fill in the multiplication table below. He wanted to look for patterns. As he was working, a rare spotted mathhopper hopped by his window. He quickly picked up his net and followed it out the window.

Help Professor Peabody with his work by finishing this table for him. Look for patterns. On a separate sheet of paper, write a report that tells Professor Peabody about the patterns you find.

x	10	20	30	40	50	60	70	80	90	100
1									90	100
2			60					160	180	
3							210	240		
4					240	280				
5					250	300				500
6				240	300					
7			210	280						
8		160	240						720	
9	90	180								
10	100									

Multiples of Tens and Hundreds   DAB · Grade 3 · Unit 11 · Lesson 8 175

Discovery Assignment Book - Page 175

AT A GLANCE

Math Facts and Daily Practice and Problems

DPP Bit S is the *Quiz on 5s and 10s.* Task T builds number sense and practices math facts.

Developing the Activity

Students complete *Questions 1–4* on the *Multiples of Tens and Hundreds* Activity Page in the *Student Guide.*

Homework

Assign the *Professor Peabody's Multiplication Table* Homework Page in the *Discovery Assignment Book.*

Assessment

1. Use DPP Bit S and the *Observational Assessment Record* to note students' fluency with the multiplication facts for the fives and tens.
2. Transfer appropriate documentation from the Unit 11 *Observational Assessment Record* to students' *Individual Assessment Record Sheets.*

Notes:

Student Guide

Questions 1–4* (SG p. 155)

1. Put a 0 to the right of the number which is being multiplied by 10. For example, $4 \times 10 = 4\underline{0}$

2. **A.** 240
   B. 370
   C. 400
   D. 3480
   E. 600
   F. 1200
   G. 3400
   H. 87,600

3. **A.** 6   **B.** 60
   C. 600   **D.** 8
   E. 80   **F.** 800
   G. 18   **H.** 180
   I. 1800   **J.** 12
   K. 120   **L.** 1200

4. **A.** 1000   **B.** 900
   C. 2400   **D.** 3500
   E. 4500   **F.** 3000

Discovery Assignment Book

Professor Peabody's Multiplication Tables (DAB p. 175)

×	10	20	30	40	50	60	70	80	90	100
1	10	20	30	40	50	60	70	80	90	100
2	20	40	60	80	100	120	140	160	180	200
3	30	60	90	120	150	180	210	240	270	300
4	40	80	120	160	200	240	280	320	360	400
5	50	100	150	200	250	300	350	400	450	500
6	60	120	180	240	300	360	420	480	540	600
7	70	140	210	280	350	420	490	560	630	700
8	80	160	240	320	400	480	560	640	720	800
9	90	180	270	360	450	540	630	720	810	900
10	100	200	300	400	500	600	700	800	900	1000

*Answers and/or discussion are included in the Lesson Guide.
**Answers for all the Home Practice in the *Discovery Assignment Book* are at the end of the unit.

Discovery Assignment Book

Part 1

Questions 1–7 (DAB p. 156)

1. 90
2. 70
3. 80
4. 18
5. 47
6. 56
7. **A.** $1.75

   B. Answers will vary. Examples: 7 quarters or 1 quarter, 5 dimes, and 20 nickels

Part 2

Questions 1–6 (DAB p. 156)

1. 1300
2. 1200
3. 1400
4. 550
5. 657
6. **A.** 189 students

   B. 495 students

Part 3

Questions 1–3 (DAB p. 157)

1. Combinations for rectangle dimensions:
   1 cm by 18 cm rectangle or 18 cm by 1 cm;
   2 cm by 9 cm rectangle or 9 cm by 2 cm;
   3 cm by 6 cm rectangle or 6 cm by 3 cm
   rectangle
2. 48
3. 10–12 sq cm

Part 4

Questions 1–3 (DAB p. 157)

1. 36 leaves
2. Answers will vary. $6 \times 3 = 18$.
3. **A.** Answers will vary. A 3-sided closed figure with 3 angles. The 3 sides come together at 3 corners.

   B. Answers will vary.

*Answers and/or discussion are included in the Lesson Guide.